William Spalding, John Hill Burton

A letter on Shakspere's authorship of the two noble kinsmen

And on the characteristics of Shakspere's style and the secret of his supremacy

William Spalding, John Hill Burton

A letter on Shakspere's authorship of the two noble kinsmen
And on the characteristics of Shakspere's style and the secret of his supremacy

ISBN/EAN: 9783742869883

Manufactured in Europe, USA, Canada, Australia, Japa

Cover: Foto ©Thomas Meinert / pixelio.de

Manufactured and distributed by brebook publishing software
(www.brebook.com)

William Spalding, John Hill Burton

A letter on Shakspere's authorship of the two noble kinsmen

A LETTER

ON

SHAKSPERE'S AUTHORSHIP

OF

𝕿𝖍𝖊 𝕿𝖜𝖔 𝕹𝖔𝖇𝖑𝖊 𝕶𝖎𝖓𝖘𝖒𝖊𝖓;

AND ON THE CHARACTERISTICS OF SHAKSPERE'S STYLE
AND THE SECRET OF HIS SUPREMACY.

BY THE LATE

WILLIAM SPALDING, M.A.,

FORMERLY PROFESSOR OF RHETORIC IN THE UNIVERSITY OF EDINBURGH, AND AFTERWARDS
PROFESSOR OF LOGIC, RHETORIC, AND METAPHYSICS IN THE UNIVERSITY OF ST
ANDREW'S ; AUTHOR OF 'A HISTORY OF ENGLISH LITERATURE,' ETC., ETC.

New Edition, with a Life of the Author,

BY

JOHN HILL BURTON, LL.D.,

AUTHOR OF
' THE HISTORY OF SCOTLAND,' ETC., ETC.

PUBLISHT FOR

The New Shakspere Society

BY N. TRÜBNER & CO., 57, 59, LUDGATE HILL,
LONDON, E.C., 1876.

FOREWORDS

THIS *Letter* by Prof. Spalding has always seemd to me one of the ablest (if not the ablest) and most stimulating pieces of Shakspere criticism I ever read. And even if you differ from the writer's conclusion as to Shakspere's part, or even hold that Shakspere took no part at all, in the Play, you still get almost as much good from the essay as if you accept its conclusions as to the authorship of *The Two Noble Kinsmen.* It is for its general, more than for its special, discussions, that I value this *Letter.* The close reasoning, the spirited language, the perception and distinction of the special qualities of Shakspere's work, the investigation into the nature of dramatic art, the grasp of subject, and the mixt logic and enthusiasm of the whole *Letter*, are worthy of a true critic of our great poet, and of the distinguisht Professor of Logic, Rhetoric, and Metaphysics, who wrote this treatise, that at once delights and informs every one who reads it. No wonder it carrid away and convict even the calm judicial mind of Hallam.

Indeed, while reading the *Letter*, one can hardly resist the power of Prof. Spalding's argument, backt as it is by his well-chosen passages from the Play. But when one turns to the play itself, when one reads it aloud with a party of friends, then come doubt and hesitation. One begins to ask, ' Is this indeed Shakspere, Shakspere at the end of his glorious career, Shakspere who has just given us Perdita, Hermione and Autolycus ' ?

Full of the heavenly beauty of Perdita's flowers, one reads over *The Two Noble Kinsmen* flower-song, and asks, pretty as the fancy of a few of the epithets is, whether all that Shakspere, with the spring-flowers of Stratford about him, and the love of nature deeper than ever in his soul —whether all he has to say of the daisy—Chaucer's ' Quene of flourës alle '— is, that it is "smelless but most quaint " ; and of marigolds, that they blow on death-beds[1], when one recollects his twenty-years' earlier

---

[1] Unsure myself as to the form of oxlip root-leaves, and knowing nothing of the use of marigolds alluded to in the lines
> "Oxlips in their cradles growing,
> Marigolds on death-beds blowing,"
also seeing no fancy even if there were fact in 'em, I applied to the best judge in England

use of them in *Lucrece* (A.D. 1594) :—

> Without the bed her other fair hand was,
> On the green coverlet; whose perfect white
> Show'd like an April *daisy* on the grass,
> With pearly sweat, resembling dew of night.
> Her eyes, like *marigolds*, had sheath'd their light,
>   And canopied in darkness sweetly lay,
>   Till they might open to adorn the day.

Full of the ineffable charm and consistency of Miranda and Perdita,
one asks of Emilia—Chaucer's daring huntress, virgin free, seeking no
marriage-bed—whether Shakspere, at the crisis of her life, degraded her
to a silly lady's-maid or shop-girl, not knowing her own mind, up and
down like a bucket in a well, balancing her lovers' qualities against one
another, saying she'd worn the losing Palamon's portrait on her right
side, not the heart one, her left, &c. ; and then (oh dear !) that Palamon
might wound Arcite and *spoil his figure.'* What a pity it would be !

> Arcite may win me,
> And yet may Palamon wound Arcite to
> The spoyling of his figure.   O what pitty
> Enough for such a chance !
>   V. iii. 68-71, p. 81, ed. Littledale.

I say, is it possible to believe that Shakspere turnd a noble lady, a
frank gallant nature, whose character he had rightly seizd at first, into a
goose of this kind, whom one would like to shake, or box her ears well ?
The thing is surely impossible.   Again, is it likely—and again, I say, at
the end of his career, with all his experience behind him, that Shakspere
would make his hero Palamon publicly urge on Venus in his prayer to
her, that she was bound to protect him because he'd believd a wanton
young wife's word that her old incapable husband was the father of her

known to me, Dr R. C. A. Prior, author of the *Popular Names of British Plants*;
and he says "I am quite at a loss for the meaning of *cradles* and *death-beds* in
the second stanza.

"The writer did not know much about plants, or he would not have combined
summer flowers, like the marigold and larkspur, with the primrose.

"I prefer the reading 'With hair-bells dimme' ; for nobody would call the
upright salver-shaped flower of the primrose a 'bell.' The poet probably means the
blue-bell."

On the other hand, Mr Wm Whale of our Egham Nurseries writes : "The root-
leaves of the Oxlip are cradle-shaped, but circular instead of long. The growth of the
leaves would certainly give one an idea of the stem and Oxlip flowers being lodged in
a cradle [? saucer].

" I have seen the marygold * in my boyish days frequently placed on coffins; and in
a warm death-room they would certainly flower. The flowers named may be all called
Spring-flowers, but of course some blowing rather later than others."

* This is called the *Calendula officinalis*, or *Medicinal Marygold*, not the African
or French sorts which are now so improved and cultivated in gardens.

child? Is this the kind of thing that the Shakspere of Imogen, of Desdemona, of Queen Catherine, would put forward as the crown of his life and work? Again I say, it can hardly be.

Further, when at one's reading-party one turns to the cleverest and most poetic-natured girl-friend, and says, 'This is assignd to Shakspere. Do you feel it's his?' She answers, 'Not a bit. And no one else does either. Look how people's eyes are all off their books. They don't care for it : you never see that when we're reading one of Shakspere's genuine plays.' Then when you note Prof. Spalding's own admission in his *Letter*, p. 81, that in Shakspere's special excellence, characterization, the play is—as of course it is—weak, and that it is to be compard on the one hand with his weaker early work, and on the other with his latest *Henry VIII*, more than half of which Fletcher wrote, you are not surpris'd to find that in 1840,[1] seven years after the date of his *Letter*, Professor Spalding had concluded, that on Shakspere's having taken part in *The Two Noble Kinsmen*, his "opinion is not now so decided as it once was," and that by 1847 he was still less decided, and declared the question "really insoluble." Here is the full passage from his article on Dyce's "Beaumont and Fletcher," in the *Edinb. Review*, July 1847, p. 57 :—

" In measuring the height of Beaumont and Fletcher, we cannot take a better scale than to put them alongside Shakespeare, and compare them with him. In this manner, an imaginary supposition may assist us in determining the nature of their excellence, and almost enable us to fix its degree. Suppose there were to be discovered, in the library of the Earl of Ellesmere, or in that of the Duke of Devonshire, two dramas not known before, and of doubtful authorship, the one being 'Hamlet,' and the other ' The Winter's Tale.' We should be at no loss, we think, to assign the former to Shakespeare : the judgment would be warranted alike by the consideration of the whole, and by a scrutiny of particular parts. But with regard to the other play, hesitation would not be at all un-reasonable. Beaumont and Fletcher (as an eminent living critic has remarked to us) might be believed to have written all its serious parts, more especially the scenes of the jealousy of Leontes, and those beautiful ones which describe the rustic festival[2]. Strange to say, a case of this kind has actually arisen. And the uncertainty which still hangs over it, agrees entirely with the hesitation which we have ventured to imagine as arising in the case we have supposed.

" In 1634, eighteen years after Beaumont's death, and nine after Fletcher's, there was printed, for the first time, the play called ' The Two Noble Kinsmen.' The bookseller in his title-page declared it to have

[1] *Edinb. Review*, July 1840, no. 144, p. 468.
[2] Surely the ' eminent living critic ' made an awful mistake about this. Beaumont and Fletcher write Perdita's flowers, Florizel's description of her, Autolycus !

been 'written by the memorable worthies of their time, Mr John Fletcher and Mr William Shakespeare, gentlemen.' On the faith of this assertion, and on the evidence afforded by the character of the work, it has been assumed universally, that Fletcher had a share in the author-ship. Shakespeare's part in it has been denied; though there is, perhaps, a preponderance of authority for the affirmative. Those who maintain the joint authorship, commonly suppose the two poets to have written together: but Mr Dyce questions this, and gives us an ingenious theory of his own, which assumes Fletcher to have taken up and altered the work long after Shakespeare's labour on it had been closed.

"*The question of Shakespeare's share in this play is really insoluble.* On the one hand, there are reasons making it very difficult to believe that he can have had any concern in it; *particularly the heavy and undramatic construction of the piece, and the want of individuality in the characters.* Besides, we encounter in it direct and palpable imitations of Shakespeare himself; among which the most prominent is the wretch-edly drawn character of the jailor's daughter. On the other hand, there are, in many passages, resemblances of expression (in the very particulars in which our two poets are most unlike Shakespeare) so close, that we must either admit Shakespeare's authorship of these parts, or suppose Fletcher or some one else to have imitated him designedly, and with very marvellous success. Among these passages, too, there are not a few which display a brilliancy of imagination, and a grasp of thought, much beyond Fletcher's ordinary pitch. Readers who lean to Mr Dyce's theory, will desire to learn his grounds for believing that Fletcher's labour in the play was performed in the latter part of his life. It appears to us that the piece bears a close likeness to those more elevated works which are known to have been among the earliest of our series: and if it were not an unbrotherly act to throw a new bone of contention among the critics, we would hint that there is no evidence entitling us peremp-torily to assert that Fletcher was concerned in the work to the exclusion of Beaumont.

"Be the authorship whose it may, 'The Two Noble Kinsmen' is un-doubtedly one of the finest dramas in the volumes before us. It contains passages which, in dramatic vigour and passion, yield hardly to any-thing—perhaps to nothing—in the whole collection; while for gorgeous-ness of imagery, for delicacy of poetic feeling, and for grace, animation, and strength of language, we doubt whether there exists, under the names of our authors, any drama that comes near to it.[1] Never has any theme enjoyed the honours which have befallen the semi-classical legend of Palamon and Arcite. Chosen as the foundation of chivalrous nar-rative by Boccaccio, Chaucer, and Dryden, it has furnished one of the

---

[1] In the *Edinburgh Review* for April 1841, p. 237-8, Prof. Spalding says that in Fletcher's *Spanish Curate,* "The scene of defiance and threatening between Jamie and Henrique is in one of Fletcher's best keys;—not unlike a similar scene in 'The Two Noble Kinsmen.'" Act III. sc. i.

fairest of the flowers that compose the dramatic crown of Fletcher, while from that flower, perhaps, leaves might be plucked to decorate another brow which needs them not.

"If the admirers of Fletcher could vindicate for him the fifth act of this play, they would entitle him to a still higher claim upon our gratitude, as the author of a series of scenes, as picturesquely conceived, and as poetically set forth, as any that our literature can boast. Dramatically considered, these scenes are very faulty: perhaps there are but two of them that have high dramatic merits—the interrupted execution of Palamon, and the preceding scene in which Emilia, left in the forest, hears the tumult of the battle, and receives successive reports of its changes and issue. But as a gallery of poetical pictures, as a cluster of images suggestive alike to the imagination and the feelings, as a cabinet of jewels whose lustre dazzles the eye and blinds it to the unskilful setting,—in this light there are few pieces comparable to the magnificent scene before the temples, where the lady and her lovers pray to the gods: and the pathetically solemn close of the drama, admirable in itself, loses only when we compare it with the death of Arcite in Chaucer's masterpiece, 'the Iliad of the middle ages.'"

All this does but show how well-founded was the judgment which that sound scholar and able Shaksperian critic, Prof. Ingram,[1] expresst in our *Transactions* for 1874, p. 454. My own words on pages 73, 64*,—written after short acquaintance with the play, and under stress of Prof. Spalding's and Mr Hickson's able Papers, and the metrical evidence—were incautiously strong. In modifying them now, I do but follow the example of Prof. Spalding himself. Little as my opinion may be worth, I wish to say that I think the metrical and æsthetic evidence are conclusive as to there being two hands in the play. I do not think the evidence that Shakspere wrote all the parts that either Prof. Spalding or Mr Hickson assigns to him, at all conclusive. If it could be shown that Beaumont[2] or any other author wrote the suppos'd Shakspere parts, and that Shakspere toucht them up, that theory would suit me best. It failing, I accept, for the time, Shakspere as the second author, subject to Fletcher having spoilt parts of his conception and work.

[1] His Dublin 'Afternoon Lecture' of 1863, shows that he then knew all that I in 1873 was trying in vain to find a known Shaksperian editor or critic to tell me.

[2] I name Beaumont because of his run-on lines, &c., and the power I find in some of the parts of his and Fletcher's joint dramas that I attribute to him.

The following scheme shows where Prof. Spalding and Mr Hickson agree, and where they differ :—

Prologue		FLETCHER (Littledale).
Act I. sc. i.	SHAKSPERE. Spalding, Hickson (Bridal Song not Sh.'s : Dowden, Nicholson, Littledale, Furnivall [1]).	
,, sc. ii.	SHAKSPERE. Spalding (Sh. revis'd by Fletcher, Dyce, Skeat, Swinburne, Littledale).	SHAKSPERE and FLETCHER, or Fletcher revis'd by Shakspere. Hickson.
,, sc. iii, iv.	SHAKSPERE. Spalding, Hickson, Littledale.	
,, sc. v.	SHAKSPERE. Spalding, ? Sh. Hickson.	? FLETCHER. Littledale.
Act II.sc. i (prose).	*SHAKSPERE. Hickson, Coleridge, Littledale.	*FLETCHER. Spalding, Dyce.
,, sc. ii, iii, iv, v, vi.		FLETCHER. Spalding, Hickson, Littledale.
Act III. sc. i.	SHAKSPERE. Spalding, Hickson.	
,, sc. ii.	*SHAKSPERE. Hickson (not Fletcher, Furnivall).	*FLETCHER. Spalding, Dyce.
,, sc. iii, iv, v, vi.		FLETCHER. Spalding, Hickson, Littledale.
Act IV. sc. i, ii.		FLETCHER. Spalding, Hickson.
,, sc. iii.	*SHAKSPERE. Hickson.	*FLETCHER. Spalding, Dyce.
Act V. sc. i (includes Weber's sc. i, ii, iii).	SHAKSPERE. Spalding, Hickson, &c.	? lines 1—17 by FLETCHER. Skeat, Littledale.
,, sc. ii.		FLETCHER. Spalding, Hickson, &c.
,, sc. iii, iv.	SHAKSPERE. Spalding, Hickson, &c., with a few lines FLETCHER. Sc. iv. (with FLETCHER interpolations. Swinburne, Littledale).	
Epilogue	·	FLETCHER. Littledale.

Mr Swinburne, when duly clothed and in his right mind, and not exposing himself in his April-Fool's cap and bells, will have something to say on the subject ; and it will no doubt be matter of controversy to the end of time. Let every one study, and be fully convinct in his own mind.

To Mrs Spalding and her family I am greatly oblig'd for their willing consent to the present reprint. To Dr John Hill Burton, the Historian of Scotland, we are all grateful for his interesting Life of his

---

[1] I cannot get over Chaucer's daisies being calld "smelless but most quaint." The epithets seem to me not only poor, but pauper : implying entire absence of fancy and imagination.—F. "Chough hoar" is as bad though.—H. L.

* Here Prof. Spalding and Mr Hickson differ.

old schoolfellow and friend, which comes before the author's *Letter*. Miss Spalding too I have to thank for help. And our Members, Mrs Bidder—the friend of our lost sweet-natured helper and friend, Richard Simpson—and Mr *****, for their gifts of £10 each, and the Rev. Stopford Brooke for his gift of four guineas, towards the cost of the present volume.

To my friend Miss Constance O'Brien I am indebted for the annext Scheme of Prof. Spalding's argument, and the Notes and Index. The side-notes, head-lines, and the additions to the original title-page[1] are mine. I only regret that the very large amount of his time—so much wanted for other pressing duties,—which Mr Harold Littledale has given to his extremely careful edition of *The Two Noble Kinsmen* for us, has thrown on me, who know the Play so much less intimately than he does, the duty of writing these *Forewords*. But we shall get his mature opinion in his Introduction to the Play in a year or two[2].

F. J. FURNIVALL.

3, St George's Square, Primrose Hill,
        London, N.W., Sept. 27—Oct. 13, 1876.

---

[1] This was "A Letter / on / Shakspeare's Authorship / of / 𝔗𝔥𝔢 𝔗𝔴𝔬 𝔑𝔬𝔟𝔩𝔢 𝔎𝔦𝔫𝔰𝔪𝔢𝔫; / a Drama commonly ascribed / to John Fletcher. / Edinburgh : / Adam and Charles Black ; / and Longman, Rees, Orme, Brown, Green, and Longman. / London. / M.DCCC.XXXIII."

[2] See the opinion of Mr J. Herbert Stack, an old *Fortnightly-Reviewer*, in the *Notes* at the end of this volume.

SKELETON OF PROF. SPALDING'S *LETTER*.

Introduction. Name of the play (p. 2). Historical evidence in favour of Shakspere's share in the play (6). Incorrectness of the first and second folios of his works (7). Internal evidence (10). Marked differences between Fletcher's and Shakspere's styles (11). Shakspere's versification (11); abruptness (11); mannerisms and repetitions (12); conciseness tending to obscurity (13); and rapid conception, opposed to Fletcher's deliberation and diffuseness (14); his distinct, if crowded, imagery, to Fletcher's vague indefiniteness (15). Shakspere's metaphors (16), classical allusions (18), reflective turn of mind (20), conceits (22), personification (25), all differ from Fletcher's manner (26).

Origin of the story of *The Two Noble Kinsmen* (26). Sketch of First Act, and reasons for assigning it to Shakspere (27). Outline of Second Act, assigned to Fletcher (35). First Scene of Third Act, Shakspere's (40); Plot of the rest (41). Fourth Act, Fletcher's (44). Description of Fifth Act, given to Shakspere, omitting one scene (45).

Points of likeness between Shakspere and contemporary dramatists (56). Impossibility of imitating him (58). Inferiority of the underplot (60). Reasons for supposing Shakspere chose the subject (62). His studies (67). Resemblance between classical and romantic poetry (69). Shakspere's plots contrasted with those of his contemporaries (73); his treatment of passion (74); unity of conception (78).

Poetical art compared with plastic (83). Greek plastic art aimed at expressing Beauty and affecting the senses (84); poetry, at expressing and affecting the mind (86); therefore poetry appeals to wider sympathies (88). Dramatic poetry the highest form of poetry (92).

Why Shakspere excelled (93). His representations of human nature both *true* and *impressive* (94); he delineated both its intellect and passion (99). His morality (101); his representations of evil (104).

Conclusion. Summary of the argument as to plot, scenic arrangements, and execution (105).

LIFE OF PROFESSOR W. SPALDING,

BY HIS SCHOOL-FELLOW AND FRIEND,

JOHN HILL BURTON, LL.D.,

AUTHOR OF 'THE HISTORY OF SCOTLAND,' ETC., ETC.

WILLIAM SPALDING was born on the 22nd of May in the year 1809, at Aberdeen. His father was a practising lawyer as a member of the Society of Advocates in that town, and held office as Procurator Fiscal of the district, or local representative of the law officers of the crown, in the investigation of crimes and the prosecution of criminals. Spalding's mother, Frances Read, was well connected among the old and influential families of the city. When he went to school, Spalding was known to be the only son of a widow. He had one sister who died in early life. Whatever delicacy of constitution he inherited seems to have come from his father's side, for his mother lived to the year 1874, and died in the house of her son's widow among her grown-up grandchildren.

Spalding had the usual school and college education of the district. He attended the elementary burgh schools for English reading, writing, and arithmetic, and passed on to Latin in the grammar school. In his day the fees for attendance in that school, whence many pupils have passed into eminence, were raised from 7s. 6d. to 10s. for each quarter of the year. Those who knew Spalding in later life, would not readily understand that as a school-boy he was noticeable for his personal beauty. His features were small and symmetrical, and his cheeks had a brilliant colour. This faded as he approached middle age, and the features lost in some measure their proportions. He had ever a grave, thoughtful, and acute face, and one of his favourite pupils records the quick glance of his keen grey eye in the active duties of his class. He was noticed in his latter years to have a resemblance to Francis and Leonard Horner, and what Sydney Smith said of the older and more distinguished of these brethren might have been said of Spalding's earnest honest face, that "the commandments were written on his forehead." When he had exhausted his five years' curriculum at the grammar school, Spalding stepped on a November morning, with some of his school-fellows, and a band of still more primitive youth, from the Aberdeenshire moorlands, and the distant highlands, to enter the open door of Marishal College, and compete for a bursary or endowment. This arena of mental gladiatorship was open to all comers, without question of age, country, or creed. The arrangement then followed—and no doubt still in use, for it has every quality of fairness and effectiveness to commend it, was this—An exercise was given out. It then consisted solely of a passage in English of considerable length, dictated to and written out by the competitors, who had to convert it into Latin. The name of each competitor was removed from his exercise, and kept by a municipal officer. A committee of sages, very unlikely to recognise any known handwriting among the multitude of papers subjected to their critical examination, sorted the exercises in the order of their merits, and then the names of the successful competitors were found. My present impression is that Spalding took the first bursary. It may have been the second or the third, for occasionally a careless inaccuracy might trip up the best scholar, but by acclamation the first place was assigned to Spalding. Indeed, in a general way, through the whole course of his education he swept the first prizes before him. When he finished the four years' curriculum of Marishal College, he attended a few classes in the college of Edinburgh, where the instruction was of another kind—less absolute teaching, but perhaps opportunities for ascending into higher spheres of knowledge. It was a little to the surprise of his companions that he was next found undergoing those " Divinity Hall " exercises, which predicate ambition to be ordained for the Church of Scotland, with the prospect, to begin with, of some moorland parish with a manse on a windy hill and a sterile but extensive glebe, a vista lying beyond of possible promotion to the ministry of some wealthy and hospitable civic community. Spalding said little about his views while he studied for the Church, and nothing about his reasons for changing his course, as he did, after a few months of study in his usual energetic fashion. He had apparently no quarrel either with institutions or persons, stimulating him to change his design, and he ever spoke respectfully of the established Church of Scotland.

From this episodical course of study he brought with him some valuable additions to the large stores of secular learning at his command. He had a powerful memory, and great facilities for mastering and simplifying sciences as well as languages. He seemed to say to himself, like Bacon, "I have taken all knowledge to be my province." With any of his friends who strayed into eccentric by-paths of inquiry he was sarcastic—almost intolerant, in denouncing their selection. Why abandon the great literature—the great sciences and the great arts—which the noblest and strongest intellects in all ages have combined to enrich and bring to perfection? Master all that has been done in these, in the first place, and then you may be permitted to take your devious course. In all the departments of study he seemed to pass over the intermediate agencies, to contemplate with something like worship the great leading spirits whose intellectual stature raised them far above the mob. So in literature, it was in Homer and Shakspeare that he delighted. In the sciences connected with the analysis and the uses of intellect, he looked to Aristotle, Hume, and Kant. In the exact sciences, to Galileo, Tycho Brache and Newton, and so on. In art, he could admit the merits of a Teniers, an Ostade, or a Morland, in accurately rendering nature, as he would admit the merit of an ingenious toy. He could not but wonder at the turbulent power of Rubens, but he was bitter on the purpose these gifts were put to, in developing unsightly masses of flesh, and motions and attitudes wanting alike in beauty and dignity. It was in Michel Angelo, Raphael, and Thorwaldsen, with a select group from those approaching near to these in their characteristic qualities, that the young student selected the gods of his idolatry.

This love of art was something new in Spalding's native district. There all forms of learning were revered, and many a striving rustic devoted the whole energies of his life to acquire the means of teaching his fellow-men from the pulpit or the printing press. But art was nought among them. Spalding was thoroughly attached to his native district, and could well have said, "I love my fathers' northern land, where the dark pine trees grow;" but when his thoughts ran on art, he would some-times bitterly call the north of Scotland a modern Bœotia. This is not the place for inquiring how it came to pass, that neglect of art could keep company with an ardent love of letters, but it is remarkable that the district so destitute of the æsthetic, gave to the world some considerable artists. In the old days there was George Jameson; and in Spalding's own generation, Bœotia produced Dyce, Giles, Philips, and Cassy as painters, with Brodie as a sculptor. Spalding could not but see merit in these, for none of them gave themselves to vulgar or purely popular art. Still he panted after the higher altitudes, and it appeared to him at one time that in his friend David Scot he had found the practical master of his ideal field. Scot had, to be sure, grand conceptions, but he did not possess the gift that enabled the great masters to abstract them from the clay of the common world. He had the defect—and his friend seeing it, felt it almost as a personal calamity—of lapsing into the ungainly, and even the grotesque, in his most aspiring efforts.

In approaching the time when the book to which this notice is prefixed was published, one is tempted to offer a word or two of explanation on its writer not appearing before the world earlier ; and when he did appear choosing so unobtrusive a fashion for his entry. About the time when his college education ended, there was something like a revival of literary ambition in Aberdeen, limited to young men who were Spalding's contemporaries. A few of them appealed for the loudest blasts of the trumpet of fame, in grand efforts in heroic and satirical poetry, and their works may be found in the libraries of collectors curious in specimens of forgotten provincial literature. These authors were generally clever young men ; and like others of their kind, they found in after life that verse was not the only path to fame or fortune. One of them became a distinguished pulpit orator. If Paley noticed, as an " only defect " in a brother clergyman, that he was a popular preacher, Spalding was apt to take a harsher view of such a failing ; nor would he palliate it on the representation of one who was the friend and admirer of both, who pleaded the trials that a person so gifted is subjected to, noting that there were certain eminences that the human head could not reach without becoming dizzy—as, for instance, being Emperor of Russia, Ambassador at an oriental court, Provost of a Scotch "Burgh toon"—or a popular preacher. Another contemporary who courted and obtained popularity, and still, to the joy of his friends, lives to enjoy it, was less distasteful to Spalding, though trespassing on his own field of ambition as a Greek scholar and Homeric critic. But he made the distinction, that in this instance he thought the homage to popularity was natural to the man, moving in irresistible impulses unregulated by a system for bringing popularity in aid of success.

The lookers-on, knowing that Spalding was ambitious, expected to hear him in the tuneful choir, but he was dumb. He was once or twice, by those nearest to him, heard in song, and literally heard only, for it is believed that he never allowed any manuscript testimony of such a weakness to leave his custody. One satirical performance got popularity by being committed to memory. It was called " The fire-balloon." In the year 1828 there was an arousing of public sympathy with the sufferers by a great conflagration at Merimachi in North America. A body of the students who had imbibed from the Professor of Natural Philosophy an enthusiasm about aerostation, proposed to raise money for the sufferers by making and exhibiting a huge fire balloon. The effort was embarrassed by many difficulties and adventures affording opportunity for the satirist.

For instance, a trial trip was attempted, and one of "the committee," who was the son of a clergyman, got hold of the key of his father's church, and put its interior at the disposal of his colleagues. The balloon inflated and ascended. The problem of getting it down again, however, had not been solved. It got itself comfortably at rest in the roof of a cupola, and the young philosophers then had to wait until it became exhausted enough to descend.

The literary ambition of young Aberdeen found for itself a very sedate and respectable looking organ in "*The Aberdeen Magazine,*" published monthly during the years 1831 and 1832, and still visible in two thick octavo volumes. Spalding was not to be tempted into this project, though there was a slight touch in it supposed, solely from internal evidence, to have come from him. A heavy controversy was begun by one calling himself "a classical reformer," who brought up foemen worthy of his steel. At the end of the whole was a sting in a postscript, more effective than anything in the unwieldy body it was attached to. "P. S. As I am no great scholar, perhaps your classical Reformer will have the goodness to tell me where I can see *The Works of Socrates.* He seems to allude to them twice [reference to pages]. As he modestly tells us that he is a much better translator of Homer than Pope was, perhaps he will be kind enough to favour the world with a translation, to use his own words, of "those works which have immortalized the name of Socrates." [1]

The papers in the Aberdeen Magazine were not all of the sombre cumbrous kind. There was an infusion of fresh young blood, fired perhaps by the influence of Wilson and Lockhart in Blackwood's Magazine, but seeking original forms of its own. For the leader of this school, Spalding had both esteem and admiration, but it was for far other merits than those of the brisk unrestrained writer of fugitive literature. This was Joseph Robertson, afterwards distinguished as an archæologist. He survived Spalding eight years. No lines of study could well be in more opposite directions than those of the two men who respected each other. While Spalding revelled in all that was brightest and best in literature and art, Robertson devoted himself to the development of our knowledge about the period when the higher arts—those of the painter and the sculptor—had been buried with the higher literature, and the classic languages had degenerated, in the hands of those who, as Du Cange, whose ample pages were often turned by Robertson, called them, were "Scriptores mediæ et infimæ Latinitatis." The source of Spalding's admiration was that Robertson's writing was perfect of its kind, and led

[1] Aberdeen Magazine, II., 350.

to important and conclusive results. It was in this spirit that he wrote his own "Letter." It did not fulfil a high aspiration, but it must be perfect ; and it was surely a moment of supreme happiness to him, when he found the unknown author sought for and praised by so cautious and reserved a critic as Hallam.

The "Letter" was published in 1833. It is characteristic of its author's distaste of loud applause, that whenever this, his first achievement in letters, saw the light, he fled, as it were, from the knowledge of what was said of it, and wandered for several months in Italy and Germany. This was an era in his life, for it gave him the opportunity of seeing face to face, and profoundly studying, the great works of art that had hitherto only been imaged in his dreams from copies and engravings. He at the same time studied—or rather enjoyed—nature. In his native north he had been accustomed to ramble among the Grampians at the head of the Dee, where the precipices are from 1500 to 2000 feet high, and snow lies all the year round. In these rambles he encountered hardships such as one would hardly have thought within the capacity of his delicate frame. He took the same method of enjoyable travelling in the Apennines—that of the Pedestrian.

He gave to the world a slight morsel descriptive of his experiences and enjoyments, in the Blackwood's Magazine of November, 1835. They were told in so fine a spirit, so free both from ungraceful levity and solemn pedantry, that the reader only regretted that they were too sparingly imparted. He thus announced his own enjoyment in his pilgrimage : "Among the ruined palaces and temples of Rome, and in the vineyards and orange-groves beside the blue sea of Naples, I had warmed my imagination with that inspiration which, once breathed upon the heart, never again grows cold. It did not desert me now as I entered this upper valley of the Apennines to seek a new colour and form of Italian landscape. Happy and elevating recollections thronged in upon me, and blended with the clear sunshine which slept on the green undulating hills." This fragment is the only morsel of autobiographic information left by its author, and therefore perhaps the following, taken from among many expressions of a genial spirit enjoying itself in freedom, may not be unacceptable. He has crossed the high-lying, bare plain of Rosetto, and reaches the village of Val san Giovanni, where "shelter was heartily welcome, the sun was set, snow-flakes were beginning to whirl in the air, and before we reached the village, a sharp snowstorm had set in." Here he is taking comfort to himself before a huge wood fire, when "a man entered of superior dress and appearance to the rest, and behind him bustled up a little wretch in the government in-direct-tax livery, who, never saying by your leave, pushed a chair to the fire for his master. The gentleman popped down, and turning to me, 'I am the Podestà,' said he. I made my bow to the chief magistrate of the place. 'I am the Potestà,' said he again, and our little squinting spy repeated reproachfully, 'His excellency is the Podestà.'

"I was resolved not to understand what they would be at, and the dignitary explained it to me with a copious use of circumlocution. He said he had no salary from the government—this did not concern me ;-- that he had it in charge to apprehend all vagabonds ; this he seemed to think might concern me. He asked for my passport, which was ex-hibited and found right ; and the Podestà proved the finest fellow possible. These villagers then became curious to know what object I had in travelling about among their mountains. My reader will by this time believe me when I say that the question puzzled me. My Atanasio felt that it touched his honour to be suspected of guiding a traveller who could not tell what he travelled for. He took on him the task of reply. Premising that I was a foreigner, and perhaps did not know how to express myself, he explained that I was one of those meritorious indi-viduals who travel about discovering all the countries and the unknown mountains, and putting all down on paper ; and these individuals always ask likewise why there are no mendicant friars in the country, and which the peasants eat oftenest, mutton or macaroni ? He added, with his characteristic determined solemnity, that he had known several such in-quisitive travellers. This clear definition gave universal satisfaction."[1]

Soon after Spalding's return to Scotland, the late George Boyd, the sagacious chief of the Firm of Oliver and Boyd, thought he might serve him in a considerable literary project. It was the age of small books published in groups—of "Constable's Miscellany," "Lardner's Cyclo-pedia," "Murray's Family Library," and the like. With these Mr Boyd thought he would compete, in the shape of the "Edinburgh Cabinet Library," and Spalding was prevailed on to write for it three volumes, with the title, "Italy and the Italian Islands." The bulk of the contributions to such collections are mere compilations. But Scott, Southey, Macintosh, and Moore had enlivened them with gifts from a higher literature, and Spalding's contribution was well fitted to match with the best of these, though he had to content himself in the ranks of the compilers, until the discerning found a higher place for his book.

The same acute observer who had set him to this task found another

[1] Blackwood's Mag., Nov. 1835, p. 669.

for him in "The History of English Literature." The *Encyclopedia Britannica* in the same manner drew him into contributions which developed themselves into two works of great value, on "Logic," and on "Rhetoric." That one of so original and self-relying a nature should have thus been led by the influence of others into the chief labours of his life, is explained by the intensity of his desire for perfection in all he did. Once induced to lift his pen in any particular cause, he could not lay it down again while there remained an incompleteness unfilled, or an imperfection unremedied.

In a review on his book on Logic, having detected, from " various internal symptoms of origin," the style and manner of a personal friend of his own, he wrote to the culprit in this characteristic form, " very many thanks for the notice. It may do good with some readers who don't know the corrupt motives by which it was prompted : and it strikes me as being exceedingly well and dexterously executed. I am quite sorry to think how much trouble it must have cost you to pierce into the bowels of the dry and dark territory, so far as the points you have been able to reach. I am afraid also that you had to gutta-percha your conscience a little, before it would stretch to some of your allegations, both about the work and about the science. I see already so much that I could myself amend—not in respect of doctrine, but in the manner of exposition—as to make me regret that I am not in a place where the classes of students are large enough to take off an edition, and so to give me by and by the chance of re-writing the book. Yet it is satisfactory to me to have got clearly the start of the publication of Hamilton's Lectures, and so to anticipate—for some of the points on which it will certainly be found that I have taken up ground of my own—the attention of *some* of the few men who have written on the science. Any of them who, having already looked into my book, shall attempt to master Hamilton's system when it appears in his own statement of it, are sure to find, if I do not greatly mistake, that I have raised several problems, the discussion of which will require that my suggestions be considered independently of Hamilton's, and my little bits of theory either accepted or refuted. I dare say I told you that early in the winter I had very satisfactory letters from Germany, and you heard that the book was kindly taken by some of the Englishmen it was sent to, and set on tooth and nail, though very amicably, by," &c.

Let us go back to the chronology of his personal history, after his one opportunity of seeing the world outside of Britain. He had joined the Bar of Scotland before this episode in his life, and on his return he took

up the position of an advocate prepared for practice.   This was no idle
ambitious attempt, for he had endured the drudgery of a solicitor's office
for the mastery of details, and had thoroughly studied the substance of
the law.   His career now promised a great future.   He was affluent
enough to spurn what Pope called "low gains;" he had good connections,
and became speedily a rising counsel.   His career seemed to be in the
line of his friend Jeffrey's, taking all the honours and emoluments of the
profession, and occasionally relaxing from it in a brilliant paper in the
Edinburgh Review.[1]   To complete the vista of good fortune he took to
be the domestic sharer of his fortunes a wife worthy of himself—Miss
Agnes Frier, born of a family long known and respected on the Border.
They were married on the 22nd of March in the year 1838.

Perhaps some inward monitor told him that the fortunes before him
were too heavy to be borne by the elements of health and strength allotted
to him.   It was to the surprise of his friends that in 1838 he abandoned
the bar, and accepted the chair of Rhetoric in Edinburgh.   In 1845 he
exchanged it for the chair of Rhetoric and Logic at St Andrews.   The
emoluments there were an inducement to him, since part of the property
of his family had been lost through commercial reverses over which he
had no control; and he was not one to leave anything connected with
the future of his family to chance.   It was a sacrifice, for he left behind
him dear friends of an older generation, such as Jeffrey, Cockburn,
Hamilton, Wilson, and Pillans.   Then there were half way between
that generation and his own, Douglas Cheape, Charles Neaves, and
George Moir ; while a small body of his contemporaries sorely missed
him, for he was a staunch friend ever to be depended on.   He was a

---

[1] The following list of her father's contributions, drawn up by Miss Mary Spalding,
is believed to be complete.

No. 144. July 1840.   Recent Shaksperian Literature.   (Books by Collier, Brown,
De Quincey, Dyce, Courtenay, C. Knight, Mrs Jameson, Coleridge, Hallam, &c.)

No. 145. October 1840.   Introduction to the Literature of Europe, by Henry
Hallam.

No. 147. April 1841.   The Works of Beaumont and Fletcher.   With an Introduction.   By George Darley.

No. 164. April 1845.   1. The Pictorial Edition of the Works of Shakespeare.
Edited by Charles Knight. — 2. The Comedies, Histories, Tragedies, and Poems
of William Shakespeare.   Edited by Charles Knight. — 3. The Works of William
Shakespeare.   The text formed from an entirely new collation of the old editions ;
with the various Readings, Notes, a Life of the Poet, and a History of the English
Stage.   By J. Payne Collier, Esquire, F.S.A.

No. 173. July 1847.   The Works of Beaumont and Fletcher.   By the Rev. Alex-
ander Dyce.

No. 181. July 1849.   1. Lectures on Shakespeare.   By H. N. Hudson. — 2.
Macbeth de Shakespeare, en 5 Actes et en vers.   Par M. Emile Deschemps.

ib. King Arthur.   By Sir E. Bulwer Lytton.   2nd edition, London, 1849, 8vo.

great teacher, and left a well-trained generation of scholars behind him. The work of the instructor, abhorred by most men, and especially by sensitive men, was to him literally the "delightful task" of the poet who has endured many a jibe for so monstrous a euphuism. Even while yet he was himself a student, if he saw that a companion was wasting good abilities in idleness or vapid reading, he would burden his own laborious hours with attempts to stimulate his lazy friend. Just after he had passed through the Greek class of Marishal College, a temporary teacher for that class was required. Some one made the bold suggestion of trying the most distinguished of the students fresh from the workshop, and Spalding taught the class with high approval. As years passed on, the spirit of the teacher strengthened within him. The traditions of the older university were more encouraging to the drilling process than Edinburgh, where the tendency was towards attractive lecturing. So entirely did the teacher's duty at last absorb his faculties, that the phenomenon was compared to the provisions in nature for compensating the loss by special weaknesses or deficiencies, and that the scholar, conscious that his own days of working were limited, instinctively felt that in imparting his stores to others who would distribute them after he was gone, he was making the most valuable use of his acquirements.

It was a mighty satisfaction to old friends in Edinburgh to hear that Spalding had condescended to seek, and that he had found, that blessed refuge of the overworked and the infirm, called a hobby. He was no sportsman. The illustrious Golfing links of St Andrews were spread before him in vain, though their attractions induced many a man to pitch his tabernacle on their border, and it was sometimes consolatorily said of Professors relegated to this arid social region, that they were reconciling themselves to Golf. The days were long past for mounting the knapsack and striding over the Apennines or even the Grampians. Spalding's hobby was a simple one, but akin to the instincts of his cultivated taste; it was exercised in his flower-garden. We may be sure that he did not debase himself to the example of the stupid floriculturist, the grand ambition of whose life is successfully to nourish some prize monster in the shape of tulip or pansy. He allied his gentle task of a cultivator of beautiful flowers, with high science, in botany and vegetable physiology.

Besides such lighter alleviations, he had all the consolations that the most satisfactory domestic conditions can administer to the sufferer. In his later days he became afflicted with painful rheumatic attacks, and the terrible symptoms of confirmed heart-disease. He died on the 16th of November, 1859.

A LETTER

ON

SHAKSPEARE'S AUTHORSHIP

OF THE DRAMA ENTITLED

THE TWO NOBLE KINSMEN.

My DEAR L——, We have met again, after an interval long enough to have made both of us graver than we were wont to be. A few of my rarely granted hours of leisure have lately been occupied in examining a question on which your taste and knowledge equally incline and qualify you to enter. Allow me to address to you the result of my inquiry, as a pledge of the gratification which has been afforded me by the renewal of our early intercourse.

Proud as SHAKSPEARE's countrymen are of his name, it is singular, though not unaccountable, that at this day our common list of his works should remain open to correction. Every one knows that some plays printed in his volumes have weak claims to that distinction ; but, while the exclusion even of works certainly not his would now be a rash exercise of prerogative in any editor, it is a question of more interest, whether there may not be dramas not yet admitted among his collected works, which have a right to be there, and might be inserted without the danger attending the dismissal of any already put upon the list. A claim for admission has been set up in favour of Malone's six plays,[1] without any ground as to five of them, and [2] with very little to support it even for the sixth. Ireland's impostures are an anomaly in literary history : even the spell and sway of temporary fashion and universal opinion are causes scarcely adequate to account for the blindness of the eminent men who fell into the snare. The want of any external evidence in favour of the

The list of SHAKSPERE'S *works is not yet settled.*

Are all his in his publisht " Works"?

Six "Doubtful Plays:" (none by Shaksper.)

Ireland's forgery, Vortigern. [c page 2]

[1] Locrine—Sir John Oldcastle—Lord Cromwell—The London Prodigal—The Puritan—The Yorkshire Tragedy.

first fabrication, the Shakspeare papers, was overlooked ; and the internal evidence, which was wholly against the genuineness, was unhesitatingly admitted as establishing it. The play of ' Vortigern ' had little more to support it than the previous imposition.

The folly of supposing Vortigern genuine.

There are two cases, however, in which we have external presumptions to proceed from ; for there are traditions traceable to Shakspeare's own time, or nearly so, of his having assisted in two plays, still known to us, but never placed among his works. The one, the ' Sejanus', in which Shakspeare is said to have assisted Jonson, was re-written by the latter himself, and published as it now stands among his writings, the part of the assistant poet having been entirely omitted ; so that the question as to that play, a very doubtful question, is not important, and hardly even curious. But the other drama is in our hands as it came from the closets of the poets, and, if Shakspeare's partial authorship were established, ought to have a place among his works. It is, as you know, THE TWO NOBLE KINSMEN, printed among the works of Beaumont and Fletcher, and sometimes attributed to SHAKSPEARE and FLETCHER jointly. I have been able to satisfy myself that it is rightly so attributed, and hope to be able to prove to you, who are intimately conversant with Shakspeare, and familiar also with the writings of his supposed co-adjutor, that there are good grounds for the opinion. The same conclusion has already been reached by others ; but the discussion of the question cannot be needless, so long as this fine drama continues excluded from the received list of Shakspeare's works ; and while there is reason to believe that there are many discerning students and zealous admirers of the poet, to whom it is known only by name. The beauty of the work itself will make much of the investigation delightful to you, even though my argument on it may seem feeble and stale.

Shakspere said (absurdly) to have helpt in

Ben Jonson's Sejanus.

The Two Noble Kinsmen attributed to Shakspere and Fletcher; and rightly so.

It is unjustly excluded from Shakspere's Works.

The proof is, of course, two-fold ; the first branch emerging [1] from any records or memorials which throw light on the subject from without ; the second, from a consideration of the work itself, and a comparison of its qualities with those of Shakspeare or Fletcher. You will keep in mind, that it has not been doubted, and may be assumed, that Fletcher had a share in the work ; the only question

I. Historical or External Evidence.
II. External Evidence, p. 10.
[¹ page 3]

is,—Whether Shakspeare wrote any part of it, and what parts, if any?

The Historical Evidence claims our attention in the first instance; but in no question of literary genuineness is this the sort of proof which yields the surest grounds of conviction. Such questions arise only under circumstances in which the external proof on either side is very weak, and the internal evidence has therefore to be continually resorted to for supplying the defects of the external. It is true that a complete proof of a work having been actually written by a particular person, destroys any contrary presumption from intrinsic marks; and, in like manner, when a train of evidence is deduced, showing it to be impossible that a work could have been written by a certain author, no internal likeness to other works of his can in the least weaken the negative conclusion. In either case, however, the historical evidence must be incontrovertible, before it can exclude examination of the internal; and the two cases are by no means equally frequent. It scarcely ever happens that there is external evidence weighty enough to establish certainly, of itself, an individual's authorship of a particular work; but the external proof that his authorship was impossible, may often be convincing and perfect, from an examination of dates, or the like. Since, therefore, external evidence against authorship admits of completeness, we are entitled, when such evidence exclusively is founded on, to demand that it shall be complete. Where by the very narrowest step it falls short of a demonstration of absolute impossibility, the internal evidence cannot be refused admittance in contravention of it, and comes in with far greater force than that of the other. There may be cases where authorship can be made out to the highest degree, at least, of probability, by strong internal evidence coming in aid of an external proof equally balanced for and against; and even where the extrinsic proof is of itself sufficient [1] to infer improbability, internal marks may be so decided the opposite way, as to render the question absolutely doubtful, or to occasion a leaning towards the affirmative side. These principles point out the internal evidence as the true ground on which my cause must be contested; but it was not necessary to follow them out to their full extent; for I can show you,

I. External Evidence.

Historical evidence cannot exclude internal, unless the former is complete.

[1 page 4]

Internal evidence the true test for *The Two N. K.*

that the external facts which we have here, few as they are, raise a presumption in favour of Shakspeare's authorship, as strong as exists in cases of more practical importance, where its effect has never been questioned.

The fact from which the maintainers of Shakspeare's share in this drama have to set out, is the first printing of it, which took place in 1634. In the title-page of this first edition,[1] the play is stated to be the joint work of Shakspeare and Fletcher. It is needless to enumerate categorically the doubts which have been thrown, chiefly by the acute and perverse Steevens, on the credit

due to this assertion; for a few observations will show that they have by no means an overwhelming force, while there are contrary presumptions far more than sufficient to weigh them down. The

edition was not published till eighteen years after Shakspeare's death, and nine years after Fletcher's; but any suspicion which might arise from the length of this interval, as giving an opportunity for imposture, is at once removed by one consideration, which is almost an unanswerable argument in favour of the assertion on the title-page, and in contravention of this or any other doubts.   There was

no motive for falsely stating Shakspeare's authorship, because no end would have been gained by it; for it is a fact admitting of the fullest proof, that, even so recently after Shakspeare's death as 1634, he had fallen much into neglect.   Fletcher had become far more popular, and his name in the title-page would have been a surer passport to public favour than Shakspeare's.   If either of the names

was to be ²fabricated, Fletcher's (which stands foremost in the title-page as printed) was the more likely of the two to have been preferred.   It appears then that the time when the publisher's assertion of Shakspeare's authorship was made, gives it a right to more confidence than it could have deserved if it had been advanced earlier. If the work had been printed during the poet's life, and the height of his popularity, its title-page would have been no evidence at all.

---

[1] "The Two Noble Kinsmen : presented at the Blackfriers, by the Kings Majesties servants, with great Applause: written by the memorable Worthies of their Time, Mr John Fletcher and Mr William Shakspeare, Gent.   Printed at London by Tho. Cotes, for John Watersone; and are to be sold at the signe of the Crowne, in Pauls Church-yard : 1634."

And when the assertion is freed from the suspicion of designed imposture, the truth of it is confirmed by its stating the play to have been acted by the king's servants, and at the Blackfriars. It was that company which had been Shakspeare's; the Globe and Blackfriars were the two theatres at which they played; and at one or the other of these houses all his acknowledged works seem to have been brought out. The fact of the play not having been printed sooner, is accounted for by the dramatic arrangements and practice of the time: the first collected edition of Shakspeare's works, only eleven years earlier than the printing of this play, contained about twenty plays of his not printed during his life; and the long interval is a reason also why the printer and publisher are different persons from any who were concerned in Shakspeare's other works. The hyperbolical phraseology of the title-page is quite in the taste of the day, and is exceeded by the quarto editions of some of Shakspeare's admitted works.

2 N. K. acted at the Blackfriars (in whose profits Shakspere had once a share).

Was the alleged co-operation then in itself likely to have taken place? It was. Such partnerships were very generally formed by the dramatists of that time; both the poets were likely enough to have projected some union of the kind, and to have chosen each other as the parties to it. Although Shakspeare seems to have followed this custom less frequently than most of his contemporaries, we have reason to think that he did not wholly refrain from it; and his favourite plan of altering plays previously written by others, is a near approach to it. As to Fletcher, his name is connected in every mind with that of Beaumont; and the memorable and melancholy letter of the three players,[1] proves him to have coalesced with other writers even during that poet's short [2] life. This is of some consequence, because, if the two poets wrote at the same time, it would seem that they must have done so previously to Beaumont's death; for Shakspeare lived only one year longer than

Custom of authors writing plays together.

Shakspere followed this custom, though rarely.

Fletcher very often.

[2 page 6]

---

[1] Gifford's Massinger, vol. i. p. xv. [Moxon's ed. p. xxxix, and *B. and Fl.* i. xiii. The letter is from Nat. Field, Rob. Daborne, and Philip Massinger, to Henslowe the manager: "You know there is x. *l.* more at least to be receavd of you for the play. We desire you to lend us v *l.* of that, which shall be allowd to you. Nat. Field." "The money shall be abated out of the money remayns for *the play of Mr. Fletcher and ours.* Rob. Daborne."—F.]

Beaumont, and is believed to have spent that year in the country. There is no proof that the drama before us was not written before Beaumont's death (1615), and it is only certain that its era was later than 1594. After the loss of his friend, Fletcher is said to have been repeatedly assisted by Massinger: he joined in one play with Jonson and Middleton, and in another with Rowley. His superior rank (he was the son of a bishop) has been gravely mentioned as discrediting his connection with Shakspeare; but the same objection applies with infinitely greater force to his known co-operation with Field, Daborne, and the others just named; and the idea is founded on radically wrong notions of the temper of that age. There is scarcely more substance in a doubt raised from the frequency with which Shakspeare is burlesqued by Beaumont and Fletcher. Those satirical flings could have been no reason why Fletcher should be unwilling to coalesce with Shakspeare, because they indicate no ill feeling towards him. They were practised by all the dramatic writers at the expense of each other; Shakspeare himself is a parodist, and indulges in those quips frequently, not against such writers only as the author of the Spanish Tragedy, but against Peele and even Marlowe, his own fathers in the drama, and both dead before he vented the jests, which he never would have uttered had he attached to them any degree of malice. And therefore also Fletcher's sarcasms cannot have disinclined Shakspeare to the coalition, especially as his personal character made it very unlikely that he should have taken up any such grudge as a testy person might have conceived from some of the more severe.

But the circumstance on which most stress has been laid as disproving Shakspeare's share in the drama in question, is this. While the first edition of it was not printed till 1634, two editions of Shakspeare's collected works had been published between the time of his death (1616) and that year, in neither of which this play appears; and it is said that its omission in the first folio (1623), in particular, is fatal to its claim, since Heminge and [1] Condell, who edited that collection, were Shakspeare's fellow-actors and the executors of his will, and must be presumed to have known perfectly what works were and what were not his. I have put this objec-

Fletcher's co-authors

His sonship to a bishop, no hindrance.

Fletcher's burlesquing Shakspere is no argument against their having written together.

Shakspere pokes fun at Kyd, Peele, Marlowe.

The 2 *N. K.* not in the First Folio of Shakspere's Works, 1623, put forth by Shakspere's fellows.
[' page 7]

tion as strongly as it can be put; and at first sight it is startling; but those who have most bibliographical knowledge of Shakspeare's works, are best aware that much of its force is only apparent. The omission in the second folio (1632) should not have been founded on; for that edition is nothing but a reprint of the contents of the first; and it is only the want of the play in this latter that we have to consider. Now, you know well, that in taking some objections to the authority of the First Folio, I shall only echo the opinions of Shakspeare's most judicious critics. It was a speculation on the part of the editors for their own advantage, either solely or in conjunction with any others, who, as holders of shares in the Globe Theatre, had an interest in the plays: for it was to the theatre, you will remark, and not to Shakspeare or his heirs personally, that the manuscripts belonged. The edition shews distinctly, that profit was its aim more than faithfulness to the memory of the poet, in the correctness either of his text or of the list of his works. Even the style of the preface excites suspicions which the work itself verifies. One object of it was to put down editions of about fifteen separate plays of Shakspeare's, previously printed in quarto, which, though in most respects more accurate than their successors, had evidently been taken from stolen copies: the preface of the folio, accordingly, strives to throw discredit on these quartos, while the text, usually close in its adherence to them, falls into errors where it quits them, and omits many very fine passages which they give, and which the modern editors have been enabled by their assistance to restore.

Here it is, however, of more consequence to notice, that the authority of the Table of Contents of the Folio is worse than weak. The editors profess to give all Shakspeare's works, and none which are not his: we know that they have fulfilled neither the one pledge nor the other. There is no doubt but they could at least have enumerated Shakspeare's works correctly: but their knowledge and their design of profit did [1]not suit each other. They have admitted, for plain reasons, two plays which are not Shakspeare's. Their edition contains about twenty plays never before printed; it was evidently their interest to enlarge this part of their list as far as they safely could. The pretended First Part of Henry VI., in

[margin notes:]
But the First Folio is not of much authority.

It was just a speculation for profit;

design to put down the Quartos,

which yet it copies.

The Table of Contents of the First Folio of Shakspere's Works is of less worth.

[1 page 8]

It lets in two Plays that are not Shakspere's.

which Shakspeare may perhaps have written a single scene,[1] but certainly not twenty lines besides, had not been printed, and could be plausibly inserted; it does not seem that they could have had any other reasons for giving it a place. The Tragedy of the Shambles, which we call 'Titus Andronicus,' if it had been printed at all, had been so only once, and that thirty years before; therefore it likewise was a novelty; and a pretext was easily found for its admission. The editors then were unscrupulous and unfair as to the works which they inserted: professing to give a full collection, they were no less so as to those which they did not insert. 'Troilus and Cressida,' an unpleasing drama, contains many passages of the highest spirit and poetical richness, and the bad in it, as well as the good, is perfectly characteristic of Shakspeare; it is unquestionably his. It does not appear in Heminge and Condell's table of contents, and is only found appended, like a separate work, to some copies of their edition. Its pages are not even numbered along with the rest of the volume; and if the first editors were the persons who printed it, it was clearly after the remainder of the work. If they did print it, their manner of doing so shews their carelessness of truth more strongly than if they had omitted it altogether. They first make up their list, and state it as a full one without that play, which they apparently had been unable to obtain; they then procure access to the manuscript, print the play, and insert it in the awkward way in which it stands, and thus virtually confess that the assertion in their preface, made in reference to their table of contents, was untrue. At any rate, a part of their impression was circulated without this play. 'Pericles' also is wholly omitted by those editors; it appears for the first time in the third folio (1666), an edition of no value, and its genuineness rests much on the internal proofs, which [2]are quite sufficient to establish it. It is an irregular and imperfect play, older in form than any of Shakspeare's; but it has clearly been augmented by many passages written by him, and therefore had a right to be inserted by the first editors, upon their own principles. These two plays then being certainly Shakspeare's, no matter whether his best or his worst, and his editors being so situated that

___

[1] Act II. Scene 4. The plucking of the roses.

It contains two plays not Shakspere's:

1 Henry VI,

and Titus Andronicus.

Troilus and Cressida

is not in the Table of Contents.

Pericles is not in the volume, and yet is in part Shakspere's.

[2 page 9]

The editors of the First Folio put forth an incomplete book.

they must have known the fact, their edition is allowed to appear as a complete collection of Shakspeare's works, although its contents include neither of the two. They probably were unable to procure copies ; but they were not the less bound to have acknowledged in their preface, that these, or any other plays which they knew to be Shakspeare's, were necessary for making up a complete collection. It in no view suited their purposes to make such a statement ; and it was not made. In short, the whole conduct of these editors inspires distrust, but their unacknowledged omission of those two plays deprives them of all claim to our confidence. The effect of that omission, in reference to any play which can be brought forward as Shakspeare's, is just this, that the want of the drama in their edition, is of itself no proof whatever that Shakspeare was not the author of it, and leaves the question, whether he was or was not, perfectly open for decision on other evidence. It leaves the inquiry before us precisely in that situation. Why Heminge and Condell could not procure the manuscripts of 'Troilus,' 'Pericles,' or the 'Two Noble Kinsmen,' I am not bound to shew. As to the last, Fletcher may have retained a partial or entire right of property in it, and was alive at the publication of their edition. Difficulties at least as great attach to the question as to the other two rejected plays, in which the strength of the other proofs has long been admitted as counterbalancing them. But the argument serves my purpose without any theory on the subject. The state of it entitles me, as I conceive, to throw the First Folio entirely out of view, as being no evidence one way or the other.

We cannot trust the Editors of the First Folio.

The First Folio no evidence against the Two Noble Kinsmen.

Laying the folio aside then, I think I have shewn that, in the most unfavourable view, no doubts which other circumstances can throw on the assertion made in the title-page of the first edition of the 'Two Noble Kinsmen,' are of such strength as to ren[1]der the truth of it improbable. Strong internal evidence therefore will, in any view, establish Shakspeare's claim. But, if the consideration first suggested be well-founded, (as I have no doubt it is,) namely, that the statement of the publisher was disinterested, there arises a very strong external presumption of the truth of his assertion, which will enable us to proceed to the examination of the internal marks with a prepossession in favour of Shakspeare's authorship.

[1 page 10]

Strong internal evidence will prove it in part Shakspere's.

As I wish to make you a convert to the affirmative opinion, it may be wise to acquaint you that you will not be alone in it, if you shall finally see reason to embrace it. Shakspeare, you know, suffered a long eclipse, which left him in obscurity till the beginning of last century, when he reappeared surrounded by his annotators, a class of men who have followed a narrow track, but yet are greater benefactors to us than we are ready to acknowledge. The commentators have given little attention to the question before us; but some of the best of them have declared incidentally for Shakspeare's claim; and though even the editors who have professed this belief have not inserted the work as his, this is only one among many evil results of the slavish system to which they all adhere. We have with us Pope, Warburton, and above all, Farmer, a man of fine discernment, and a most cautious sifter of evidence. The subject has more recently been treated shortly by a celebrated foreign critic, the enthusiastic and eloquent Schlegel,[1] who comes to a conclusion decidedly favourable to Shakspeare.

[margin note: Early annotators on Shakspere narrow-minded.]

[margin note: Yet Pope, Warburton, Farmer, believe The Two Noble Kinsmen genuine: so does Schlegel.]

There still lies before us the principal part of our task, that of applying to the presumption resulting from the external proof, (whatever the amount of that may be,) the decisive test of the [2]Internal Evidence. Do you doubt the efficacy of this supposed crucial experiment? It is true that internal similarities form almost a valueless test when applied to inferior writers; because in them the distinctive marks are too weak to be easily traced. But, in the first place, great authors have in their very greatness the pledge of something peculiar which shall identify their works, and consequently the test is usually satisfactory in its application to them; and, secondly and particularly, Shakspeare is, of all writers that have existed, that one to whose alleged works such a test can be most confidently administered; because he is not only strikingly

[margin note: II. Internal evidence.]

[margin note: [page 11]]*

[margin note: Shakspere's work specially fit for the Internal Evidence test.]

---

[1] Lectures on Dramatic Art and Literature. It would ill become me to carp at an author whom I have expressly to thank for much assistance in this inquiry, and to whom I am perhaps indebted for more than my recollection suggests. But it must be owned, that M. Schlegel's opinion loses somewhat of its weight from the fact, that he also advocates Shakspeare's authorship of some of Malone's plays, a decision in which it is neither desirable nor likely that the poet's countrymen should acquiesce.

peculiar in those qualities which discriminate him from other poets, but his writings also possess singularities, different from, and opposite to, the usual character of poetry itself.

I cannot proceed with you to the work itself, till I have reminded you of some distinctive differences between the two writers whose claims we are to adjust, the recollection of which will be indispensable to us in considering the details of the drama. We shall then enter on that detailed examination, keeping those distinctions in mind, and attempting to apply them to individual passages ; and, when all the scenes of the play have thus passed successively before us, we shall be able to look back on it as a whole, and investigate its general qualities.

Differences between Shakspere and Fletcher to be discusst.

The first difference which may be pointed out between Shakspeare and Fletcher, is that of their versification. You have learned from a study of the poets themselves, in what that difference consists. Shakspeare's versification is broken and full of pauses, he is sparing of double terminations to his verses, and has a marked fondness for ending speeches or scenes with hemi-stitches. Fletcher's rhythm is of a newer and smoother cast, often keeping the lines distinct and without breaks through whole speeches, abounding in double endings, and very seldom leaving a line incomplete at the end of a sentence or scene.[1] And the opposite taste of the two poets in their choice and arrangement [2]of words, gives an opposite character to the whole modulation of their verses. Fletcher's is sweet and flowing, and peculiarly fitted either for declamation or the softness of sorrow : Shakspeare's ear is tuned to the stateliest solemnity of thought, or the abruptness and vehemence of passion. The present drama exhibits in whole scenes the qualities of Shakspeare's versification ; and there are other scenes which are marked by those of Fletcher's ; the difference is one reason for separating the authorship.

Shakspere's and Fletcher's versification contrasted.

Shakspere's.

Fletcher's.

[2 page 12]

Modulation of Fletcher's verse : of Shakspere's.

You will notice in this play many instances of Shakspeare's favourite images, and of his very words. Is this a proof of the play having been his work, or does it only indicate imitation ? In

Shakspere's images and words in The Two Noble Kinsmen.

---

[1] Weber's Beaumont and Fletcher, vol. xiii., and Lamb, as there quoted.

Shakspeare's case, such resemblance, taken by itself, can operate neither way. Shakspeare is a mannerist in style. He knew this himself, and what he says of his minor poems, is equally true of his dramatic language ; he "keeps invention in a noted weed[1] ; " and almost every word or combination of words is so marked in its character that its author is known at a glance. But not only is his style so peculiar in its general qualities, as scarcely to admit of being mistaken ; not only is it deficient in variety of structure, but it is in a particular degree characterised by a frequent recurrence of the same images, often clothed in identically the same words. You are quite aware of this, and those who are not, may be convinced of it by opening any page of the annotated editions. So far, then, this play is only like Shakspeare's acknowledged works. It is true, that one who wished to write a play in Shakspeare's manner, would probably have repeated his images and words as they are repeated here ; but Shakspeare would certainly have imitated himself quite as often. The resemblance could be founded on, as indicating imitation, only in conjunction with other circumstances of dissimilarity or inferiority to his genuine writings ; and where, as in the present case, there seems to be reason for asserting that the accompanying circumstances point the work out as an original composition of his, this very likeness and repetition become a strong argument in support of those concomitant indications. [2]Such repetition is more or less common in all the play-writers of that age. The number of their works, the quickness with which they were written, and the carelessness which circumstances induced as to their elaboration or final correction, all aided in giving rise to this. But all are not equally chargeable with it ; Beaumont and Fletcher less than most, Massinger to an extent far beyond Shakspeare, and vying with the common-places of Euripides. May not the professional habits of Shakspeare and Massinger as actors, have had some effect in producing this, by imprinting their own works in their memories with unusual strength ? Fletcher and his associate were free from that risk.

It would not be easy to give a systematic account of those

Marginal notes:

Shakspere a mannerist in style, and

wanting in variety.
Shakspere repeats himself.

The likeness to Shakspere in *The Two Noble Kinsmen*, and the repetitions of him, are likely to be by him.

[² page 13]

Massinger also repeats himself much.

Fletcher but little.

---

[1] Sonnet 76.

qualities which combine to constitute Shakspeare's singularity of
style. Some of them lie at the very surface, others are found only
on a deeper search, and a few there are which depend on evanescent
relations, instinctively perceptible to the congenial poetical sense,
but extremely difficult of abstract prose definition. Several qualities
also, which we are apt to think exclusively his, (such, for instance,
as his looseness of construction,) are discovered on examination to
be common to him with the other dramatic writers of his age. Such
qualities can give no assistance in an inquiry like ours, and may be
left wholly out of view. But I think the distinctions which I can
specify between him and Fletcher are quite enough, and applicable
with sufficient closeness to this drama, for making out the point
which I wish to prove.

Singularity of Shakspere's style.

No one is ignorant that Shakspeare is concise, that this quality
makes him always energetic and often most impressive, but that it
also gives birth to much obscurity. He shows a constant wish to
deliver thought, fancy, and feeling, in the fewest words possible.
Even his images are brief; they are continual, and they crowd and
confuse one another; the well-springs of his imagination boil up
every moment, and the readiness with which they throw up their
golden sands, makes him careless of fitly using the wealth thus
profusely rendered. He abounds in hinted descriptions, in sketches
of imagery, in glimpses of illustration, in abrupt and vanishing
snatches of fancy. But the merest hint that he gives is of force
[1]enough to shew that the image was fully present with him; if he
fails to bring it as distinctly before us, it is either from the haste
with which he passes to another, or from the eagerness induced by
the very force and quickness with which he has conceived the
former. It has been said of Milton that language sunk under him;
and it is true of him in one sense, but of Shakspeare in two.
Shakspeare's strength of conception, to which, not less than to
Milton's, existing language was inadequate, compelled him either to
use old words in unusual meanings, or to coin new words for himself.[2] But his mind had another quality powerful over his style,

Qualities of Shakspere's style: energy, obscurity, abruptness, brevity (in late plays).

Shakspere never vague. [1 page 14]

Milton and language.

Shakspere's new meanings and new words.

[2] There are numerous instances of both these effects in the play before us.
" *Counter-reflect* (a noun) ; *meditance* ; *couch* and *corslet* (used as verbs) ; *operance* ;

Milton slow,

Shakspere rapid,

specially in reflective passages.

He forces speech to bear a burden beyond its strength.

Shakspere's obscurity.

[¹ page 15]

Fletcher most unlike Shakspere.

Fletcher diffuse.

He amplifies, is elaborate, not vigorous.

which Milton's wanted. Milton's conception was comparatively slow, and allowed him time for deliberate expression : Shakspeare's was rapid to excess, and hurried his words after it. When a truth presented itself to his mind, all its qualities burst in upon him at once, and his instantaneousness of conception could be represented only by words as brief and quick as thought itself. This cause operates with the greatest force on his passages of reflection ; for if his images are often brief, his apophthegms are brief a thousand times oftener : his quickness of ideas seems to have been stimulated to an extraordinary degree by the contemplation of general truths. And everywhere his incessant activity and quickness, both of intellect and fancy, engaged him in a continual struggle with speech ; it is a sluggish slave which he would force to bear a burden beyond its strength, a weary courser which he would urge at a speed to which it is unequal. He fails only from insufficiency in his puny instrument ; not because his conception is indistinct, but because it is too full, energetic, and rapid, to receive adequate expression. It is excess of strength which hurts, not weakness which incapacitates ; he is injured by the undue prevalence of the good principle, not by its defect. The obscurity of other writers is often the mistiness of the evening twilight sinking into night ; his is the fitful dimness of the dawn, contending with the retiring darkness, and striving to break out ¹into open day. Scarcely any writer of Shakspeare's class, or of any other, comes near him either in the faults or the grandeur which are the alternate results of this tendency of mind ; but none is more utterly unlike him than the poet to whom, some would say, we must attribute passages in this play so singularly like Shakspeare. Fletcher is diffuse both in his leading thoughts and in his illustrations. His intellect did not present truth to him with the instant conviction which it poured on Shakspeare, and his fancy did not force imagery on him with a profusion which might have tempted him to weave its different suggestions into inconsistent forms ; he expresses thought deliberately and with amplification ; he paints his illustrative pictures with a careful hand and by repeated touches ;

appointment, for military accoutrements ; *globy eyes ; scurril ; disroot ; dis-seat,*" &c. *Weber.*

his style has a pleasing and delicate air which is any thing but vigorous, and often reaches the verge of feebleness.   Take a passage or two from the work before us, and do you say, who know Fletcher, whether they be his, or the work of a stronger hand.

He only áttributes
The faculties of other instruments
To his own nerves and act; commands men's ser|vice,
And what they gain in't, boot and glory too.
.   .   .   .   What man
Thirds his own worth, (the case is each of ours,)
When that his action's dregged with mind assured
'Tis bad he goes about?—Act I. scene ii.

*Shakspere.
Fletch r
could not have
written th ये
passages,*

Dowagers, take hands :
Let us be widows to our woes : Delay
Commends us to a famishing hope.—Act I. scene i.

[t. i. *mourn them
ever*]

I do not quote these lines for praise.   The meaning of the last quotation in particular is obscure when it stands alone, and not too clear even when it is read in the scene.   But I ask you, whether the oracular brevity of each of the sentences is not perfectly in the manner of Shakspeare.   A fragment from another beautiful address in the first scene is equally characteristic and less faulty :—

*with their
oracular brevity.*

[1] Honoured Hippolita,
Most dreaded Amazonian, that hast slain
The scythe-tusked boar ; that, with thy arm as strong
As it is white, wast near to make the male
To thy sex captive, but that this thy lord
(*Born to uphold creation in that hon|our
First Nature styled it in*) shrunk thee in|to
The bound thou wast o'erflow|ing, | at once subdu|ing |
Thy force and thy affection ;—Soldieress !
That equally canst poise sternness with pit|y ;—
Who now, I know, hast much more power o'er | him
Than e'er he had on thee ;—*who owest his strength
And his love too, who is a servant to
The tenor of thy speech !*   .   .

[1 page 16]

*Shakspere, not
Fletcher.*

[*ownest*]

Is this like Fletcher? I think not.   It is unlike him in versification and in the tone of thought; and you will here particularly notice

that it is unlike him in abruptness and brevity.   It is like Shakspeare
in all these particulars.

I have said that Shakspeare, often obscure, is scarcely ever
vague ; that he may fail to express all he wishes, but almost always
gives distinctly the part which he is able to convey.   Fletcher is not

only slow in his ideas, but often vague and deficient in precision.
The following lines are taken from a scene in the play under our
notice, which clearly is not Shakspeare's.   I would direct your
attention, not to the remoteness of the last conceit, but to the want
of distinctness in grasping images, and the inability to see fully
either their picturesque or their poetical relations.

Arcite. We were not bred to talk, man : when we are armed,
And both upon our guards, then *let our fur|y,*
Like meeting of two tides, fly strongly from | us.

Palamon. Methinks this armour's very like that, Ar|cite,
Thou worest that day the three kings fell, but light|er.
Arc. That was a very good one ; and that day,
I well remember, you out-did me, cous|in:
            When I saw you charge first,
Methought I heard a dreadful clap of thund'er
Break from the troop.
Pal.   *But still before that flew*
The lightning of your valour.—Act III. scene vi.

[1] Shakspeare's style, as every one knows, is metaphorical to excess.
His imagination is always active, but he seldom pauses to indulge it
by lengthened description.   I shall hereafter have occasion to direct
your observation to the sobriety with which he preserves imagination
in its proper station, as only the minister and interpreter of thought ;
but what I wish now to say is, that in him the two powers operate

simultaneously.   He goes on thinking vigorously, while his imagination scatters her inexhaustible treasures like flowers on the current
of his meditations.   His constant aim is the expression of facts,
passions, or opinions ; and his intellect is constantly occupied in the
investigation of such ; but the mind acts with ease in its lofty voca-
tion, and the beautiful and the grand rise up voluntarily to do him
homage.   He never indeed consents to express those poetical ideas
by themselves ; but he shows that he felt their import and their

legitimate use, by wedding them to the thoughts in which they originated. The truths which he taught, received magnificence and amenity from the illustrative forms; and the poetical images were elevated into a higher sphere of associations by the dignity of the principles which they were applied to adorn. Something like this is always the true function of the imagination in poetry, and dramatic poetry in particular; and it is also the test which tries the presence of the faculty; metaphor indicates its strength, and simile its weakness. Nothing can be more different from this, or farther inferior to it, than the style of a poet who turns aside in search of description, and indulges in simile preferably to the brevity of metaphor, to whom perhaps a poetical picture originally suggested itself as the decoration of a striking thought, but who allowed himself to be captivated by the beauty of the suggested image, till he forgot the thought which had given it birth, and on its connexion with which its highest excellence depended. Such was Fletcher, whose style is poor in metaphor. His descriptions are sometimes beautifully romantic; but even then the effect of the whole is often picturesque rather than poetically touching; and it is evident that lengthened description can still less frequently be dramatic. In his descriptions, it is observable that the poetical relations introduced in illustration [1]are usually few, the character of the leading subject being relied on for producing the poetical effect. Fletcher's longest descriptions are but elegant outlines; Shakspeare's briefest metaphors are often finished paintings. Where Shakspeare is guilty of detailed description, he is very often laboured, cold, and involved; but his illustrative ideas are invariably copious, and it is often their superfluity which chiefly tends to mar the general effect. In the play that you are to examine, you will find a profusion of metaphor, which is undoubtedly the offspring of a different mind from Fletcher's; and both its excellence and its peculiarity of character seem to me to stamp it as Shakspeare's. I think the following passage cannot be mistaken, though the beginning is difficult, and the text perhaps incorrect.

> They two have *cab|in:d*
> In many as dangerous, as poor a corn|er—

Shakspere's truths and their imagery glorify one another.

Metaphor the strength of poetry; simile its weakness.

Fletcher is diffuse in description and simile,

loses the original thought in it,

is poor in metaphor, and picturesque.

[1 page 18]

Fletcher's and Shakspere's descriptions contrasted.

Metaphor in *The Two Noble Kinsmen*

is Shakspere's.

Instances of

Peril and want contending, they have *skiffed*
Torrents, whose raging *tyranny* and *power*
I' the least of these was dreadful ; and they have
Fought out together where *Death's self* was *lodged*,
Yet FATE hath BROUGHT THEM OFF. Their *knot* of love,
Tied, *weaved*, ENTANGLED, with so true, so long,
And with a *finger* of so deep a cun|ning,
May be *outworn*, never *undone*. I think
Theseus cannot be *umpire* to himself,
Cleaving his conscience into twain, and do|ing
Each side like justice, which he loves best.—Act I. scene iii.

The play throughout will give you metaphors, like Shakspeare's in
their frequency, like his in their tone and character, and like his in
their occasional obscurity and blending together.

We have been looking to Shakspeare's imagery. You will meet
with classical images in the 'The Two Noble Kinsmen.' Do not
allow any ill-applied notion of his want of learning to convert this
into an argument against his authorship. You will recollect, that an
attachment of this sort is very perceptible in Shakspeare's dramas,
and pervades the whole thread of his youthful poems. It is indeed
a prominent quality in the school of poetry, which prevailed during
the earlier part of his life, perhaps during the whole of it. In his

early days, the study of ¹Grecian and Latin literature in England
may be said to have only commenced, and the scenery and figures
of the classical mythology broke on the view of the student with

all the force of novelty. All the literature of that period is tinged
with classicism to a degree which in our satiated times is apt to
seem pedantic. It infected writers of all kinds and classes : trans-
lations were multiplied, and a familiarity with classical tales and
history was sought after or affected even by those who had no
access to the original language. Shakspeare clearly stood in this
latter predicament, his knowledge of Latin certainly not exceeding
that of a schoolboy : but the translated classics enabled him to
acquire the facts, and he shared the taste of the age to its full
extent. His admiration of the classical writers is vouched by the

subjects and execution of his early poems, by numerous allusions in
his dramas, particularly his histories, by the subjects chosen for some

of his plays, by one or two imitations of the translated Latin poets,[1] and by many exotic forms in his language, derived from the same secondary source.   Correct tameness is the usual character of classical allusion in authors well versed in classical studies.   Even Milton, who has drawn the most exquisite images of this kind, has sometimes remembered only, where he should have invented : and Fletcher, whom we have especially to consider, is no exception to the rule ; his many classical illustrations are invariably cold and poor. Shakspeare's mythological images have something singular in them. They are incorrect as transcripts of the originals, but admirable if examined without such reference ; they are highly-coloured paintings whose subjects are taken from the simplicity of some antique statue. The 'Venus and Adonis' has some fine and some overcharged pictures thus formed from the hints which he derived from his books.[2]   He received the mythological images but imperfectly, and his fancy was stimulated without being [3]clogged.   He stood but at the entrance of those visionary forests, within whose glades the heroes and divinities of ancient faith reposed ; he looked through a glimmering and uncertain light, and caught only glimpses of the sanctity of that world of wonders : and it was with an imagination heated by the flame of mystery and partial ignorance that he turned away from the scene so imperfectly revealed, to brood on the beauty of its broken contours, and allow fancy to create magnificence richer than memory ever saw. The occurrence of classical allusions here, therefore, affords no reason for doubting his authorship even of those passages in which they are found : and if we could trace any of his singularities in the images which we have, the argument in his favour would be strengthened by these.   Most of the allusions are too slightly sketched to permit this ; but one or two are like him in their unfaithfulness. We have "Mars' drum" in the 'Venus and Adonis' ; and here beauty is described as able to make him spurn it : the altar of the same

Milton's classical allusions.

Fletcher's.

Shakspere's treatment of mythology.

His Venus and Adonis.

Shakspere's treatment of classical mythology ;

[3 page 20]

---

[1] Farmer's Essay on the Learning of Shakspeare.

[2] A singularly rich and energetic piece of colouring in this sort is near the beginning of the poem, commencing,

> I have been wooed, as I entreat thee now,
> Even by the stern and direful God of War —

and extending through three stanzas.

deity is alluded to as the scene of a Grecian marriage. The " Ne-
mean lion's hide " is here, as his nerve in ' Hamlet.' But the most
specially in
Arcite's prayer in
Act V. scene i. characteristic use of this sort of imagery is in the prayer in the first
scene of the Fifth Act. The whole tenor of the language, the solemn-
ity and majesty of the tone of thought, the piling up of the heap of
metaphors and images, and the boldness and admirable originality of
This scene is
certainly
Shakspere's. their conception, all these are Shakspeare's : and the fact of this accu-
mulation of feeling, thought, and imagination, being employed to
create, out of a fragmentary classical outline, a picture both new in
its features and gorgeously magnificent in its filling up, is strongly
indicative of his hand, and strikingly resembles his mode of dealing
with such subjects elsewhere.

You will be furnished with a rule to guide your decision on
many passages of the drama otherwise doubtful, by having your
notice slightly directed to what will fall more properly under our
consideration when we look back on the general scope of the play,
Shakspere's
tendency to
reflection. —I mean Shakspeare's prevailing tendency to reflection. The
presence of a spirit of active and inquiring thought through every
page of his writings is too evident to require any proof. It is exerted on every object which comes under his notice : it is serious
[¹ page 21] when its theme is lofty ; and when the subject is familiar, ¹it is con-
His own active
and inquiring
thought, is the
only quality of
his own that he's
given all his
characters. tented to be shrewd. He has impressed no other of his own
mental qualities on all his characters : this quality colours every one
of them. It is one to which poetry is apt to give a very subordinate place : and, in most poets, fancy is the predominating power ;
because, immeasurably as that faculty in them is beneath its unequalled warmth in Shakspeare, yet intellect in them is comparatively even weaker. With inferior poets, particularly the
dramatic, inflation of feeling and profusion of imagery are the
Fletcher's
thought, small
beside
Shakspere's. alternate disguises which conceal poverty of thought. Fletcher is a
poet of much and sterling merit ; but his fund of thought is small
indeed when placed beside Shakspeare's. He has, indeed, very
Shakspere's
worldly wisdom,
and solemn
thought. little of Shakspeare's practical, searching, worldly wisdom, and none
of that solemnity of thought with which he penetrates into his
loftier themes of reflection. This quality in Shakspeare is usually
relieved by poetical decoration : Imagination is active powerfully

and unceasingly, but she is rebuked by the presence of a mightier influence ; she is but the handmaid of the active and piercing Understanding ; and the images which are her offspring serve but as the breeze to the river, which stirs and ripples its surface, but is not the power which impels its waters to the sea. As you go through this drama, you will not only find a sobriety of tone pervading the more important parts of it, but activity of intellect constantly exerted. But what demands particular notice is, the mass of general truths, of practical, moral, or philosophical maxims, which, issuing from this reflective turn of mind, are scattered through Shakspeare's writings as thick as the stars in heaven. The occurrence of them is characteristic of his temper of mind ; and there is something marked in the manner of the adages themselves. They are often solemn, usually grave, but always pointed, compressed, and energetic ;—they vary in subject, from familiar facts and rules for social life to the enunciation of philosophical truths and the exposition of moral duty. You will meet with them in this drama in all their shapes and in every page [of Shakspere's part of it].

Shakspeare's reach and comprehension of thought is as remarkable as its activity, while Fletcher's is by no means great, and in this respect Massinger comes much nearer to him. The simplest fact has many dependent qualities, and may be related by 'men of different degrees of intellect with circumstances differing infinitely, a confined mind seeing only its plainest qualities, while a stronger one grasps and combines many distant relations. Shakspeare's love of brevity would not have produced obscurity nearly so often, had it not been aided by his width of mental vision. There are many passages in the play before us which seem to emanate from a mind of more comprehension than Fletcher's. Look at the following lines. The idea to be expressed was a very simple one. Hippolita is entreating her husband to leave her, and depart to succour the distressed ladies who kneel at her feet and his ; and she wishes to say, that though, as a bride, she was loth to lose her husband's presence, yet she felt that she should act blameably if she detained him. Fletcher would have expressed no idea beyond that ; but on it alone he would have employed six lines and two or three com-

Shakspere's Imagination the handmaid of his Understanding.

Note the mass of general truths and maxims in this part of The Two Noble Kinsmen.

Shakspere's reach of thought.

[¹ page 22]

Passages in The Two Noble Kinsmen too comprehensive for Fletcher.

parisons. Hear how many cognate ideas present themselves to Shakspeare's mind in expressing the thought. The passage is obscure, but not the less like Shakspeare on that account.

> Though much unlike|ly
> I should be so transported, *as much sor|ry*
> *I should be such a suitor;* yet I think,
> Did I not, by the abstaining of my joy,
> *Which breeds a deeper longing,* cure the sur'feit
> *That craves a present medicine,* I should pluck
> All ladies' scandal on me—Act I. scene i.

It would be well if Shakspeare's continual inclination to thought gave rise to no worse faults than occasional obscurity. It was not to be hoped that it should not produce others. His tone of thinking could not be always high and serious ; and even when it flowed in a lofty channel, its uninterrupted stream could not always

be pure. His judgment often fails to perform its part, and he is guilty of conceit and quibble, not merely in his comic vein, but in his most deeply tragical situations. He has indeed one powerful excuse ; he had universal example in both respects to justify or betray him. But he has likewise another plea, that his constant activity of mind, and the wideness of its province, exposed him to

peculiar risks. A mind always in action must sometimes act wrongly ; and the constant exercise of the creative powers of the mind dulls the edge of the corrective. It was not strange that he who was unwearied in tracing the manifestations of that spirit of likeness which pervades nature, should often mistake a resemblance in name for a community of essence,—that he whose mind was sensible to the most delicate differences, should sometimes fancy he saw distinction where there was none ;—it was not strange, however much to be regretted, that he who left the smooth green slopes of fancy to clamber among the craggy steeps of thought, should often stumble in his dizzy track, either in looking up to the perilous heights above,

or downwards on the morning landscape beneath him. While the most glaring errors of the tropical Euphues are strained allegorical

conceits, Shakspeare's fault is oftener the devising of subtle and unreal distinctions, or the ringing of fantastical changes upon words.

Lily's error was one merely of taste ; Shakspeare's was one of the
judgment, and the heavier of the two, but still the error of a
stronger mind than the other ; for the judgment cannot act till the
understanding has given it materials to work upon, and those fanciful writers who do not reflect at all, are in no danger of reflecting
wrongly.   Shakspeare's evil genius triumphs when it tempts him to   Shakspere's evil genius triumphs in his puns.
a pun—it enjoys a less complete but more frequent victory in
suggesting an antithesis ; but it often happens that this dangerous
turn of mind does not carry him so far as to be of evil consequence.
It aids its quickness and directness of mental view, in giving to his
style a pointed epigrammatic terseness which is quite its own, and a
frequent weight and effect which no other equals.   Where, however,
this antithetic tendency is allowed to approach the serious scenes,
it throws over them an icy air which is very injurious, while it often
gives the comic ones a ponderousness which is altogether singular,
and but imperfectly accordant with the nature of comic dialogue.
The arrows of Shakspeare's wit are not the lightly feathered shafts   Characteristics of his wit.
which Fletcher discharges, and as little are they the iron-headed
bolts which fill the quiver of Jonson ; but they are weapons forged
from materials unknown to the others, and in an armoury to which
they had no access ; their execution is [1]resistless when they reach   [1 page 24]
their aim, but they are covered with a golden massiveness of decoration which sometimes impedes the swiftness of their flight.
But whether the effect of these peculiarities of Shakspeare be good
or evil, their use in helping an identification of his manner is very
great.   Nothing can be more directly opposite to them than the   Contrast with Fletcher's.
slow elegance and want of pointedness which we find in Fletcher,
who is not free from conceits, but does not express them with
Shakspeare's hard quaintness, while he is comparatively quite guiltless of plays on words.   The following instances are only a few
among many in the present drama, which seem to be perfectly in
Shakspeare's manner, and to most of which Fletcher's works could
certainly furnish no parallel, either in subject or in expression.

> Oh, my petition was
> Set down in ice, which, by hot grief uncan|died,   Passages by Shakspere, not Fletcher.
> Melts into tears ; so sorrow, wanting form,
> Is pressed with deeper matter.—Act I. scene i.

Theseus speaks thus of the Kinsmen lying before him in the field of battle desperately wounded :—

[The | is to show
the double
endings.]

Rather than have them
Freed of this plight, and in their morning state,
Sound and at liberty, I would them dead :
But forty thousand fold we had rather have | them
Prisoners to us than Death.   Bear them speedi|ly
From *our kind air, to them unkind,* and min|ister
What man to man may do.—Act I. scene iv.

Shakspere metaphors.

A lady hunting is addressed in this strain :

Oh jewel
O' the wood, O' the world !—Act III. scene i.

In the same scene one knight says to another,—

Shakspere
metaphor.

This question sick between us,
By bleeding must be cured.

[1 page 25]

[1] And the one, left in the wood, says to the other, who goes to the presence of the lady whom both love—

You talk of feeding me, to breed me strength ;
You are going now to look upon a sun,
That strengthens what *it* looks on.—Act III. scene i.

The two knights, about to meet in battle, address each other in these words :—

Pal.   Think you but thus ;
That there were aught in me which strove to shew
Mine enemy in this business,—were't one eye
Against another, arm opposed by arm,
I would destroy the offender ;—coz, I would,
Though parcel of myself : then from this, gath|er
How I should tender you !
Arc.   I am in la|bour
To push your name, your ancient love, our kin|dred,
Out of my memory, and i' the self-same place
To seat something I would confound.—Act V. scene i.

And afterwards their lady-love, listening to the noise of the fight, speaks thus :—

Shakspere
metaphor.

Each stroke laments
The place whereon it falls, and sounds more like
A bell than blade.—Act V. scene v.

Shakspeare's fondness for thought, the tendency of that train of thought to run into the abstract, and his burning imagination, have united in producing another quality which strongly marks his style, and is more pleasing than those last noticed.   He abounds in Personification, and delights particularly in personifications of mental powers, passions, and relations.   This metaphysico-poetical mood of musing tinges his miscellaneous poems deeply, especially the Venus and Adonis, which is almost lyrical throughout; and even in his dramas the style is often like one of Collins's exquisite odes.   This quality is common to him with the narrative poets of his age, from whom [1]he received it ; but it is adopted to no material extent by any of his dramatic contemporaries, and by Fletcher less than any.   The other dramatists, indeed, are full of metaphysical expressions, of the names of affections and faculties of the soul ; but they do not go on as Shakspere's kindling fancy impelled him to do, to look on them as independent and energetic existences.   This figure is one of the most common means by which he elevates himself into the tragic and poetic sphere, the compromise between his reason and his imagination, the felicitous mode by which he reconciles his fondness for abstract thought, with his allegiance to the genius of poetry.   'The Two Noble Kinsmen' is rich in personifications both of mental qualities and others, which have all Shakspeare's tokens about them, and vary infinitely, from the uncompleted hint to the perfected portrait.

Oh Grief and Time,
Fearful consumers, you will all devour !—Act I. scene i.

Peace might purge
For her repletion, and retain anew
Her charitable heart, now hard, and harsh|er
Than Strife or War could be.—Act I. scene ii.

A most unbounded tyrant, whose success
Makes heaven unfeared, and villainy assured
Beyond its power there's nothing,—almost puts
Faith in a fev|er,| and deifies alone
Voluble Chance.—Act I. scene ii.

This funeral path brings to your household graves ;
Joy seize on you again—Peace sleep with him !
Act I. scene v.

Marginal notes: Shakspere's personification of mental powers, passions. — In *Venus and Adonis.* — [1 page 26] — Fletcher uses it but little. — Shakspere's distinctive use of Personification. — The *Two Noble Kinsmen* is rich in personifications which must be Shakspere's. — Instances of these.

> Content and Ang|er
> In me have but one face.—Act III. scene i.

> Force and great Feat
> Must put my garland on, where she will stick
> The queen of flowers.—Act V. scene i.

Instances of Shakspere's Personification in The Two Noble Kinsmen.

[¹ page 27]

> Thou (*Love*) mayst force the king
> To be his subject's vassal, and *induce*
> *Stale Gravity to dance ;*—the pollèd bachelor,
> *Whose youth*, (like wanton boys through bon|fires,)
> ¹ *Has skipt thy flame*, at seventy thou canst catch,
> And make him, to the scorn of his hoarse throat,
> Abuse young lays of love.—Act V. scene ii.

> Mercy and manly Cour|age
> Are bed-fellows in his visage.—Act V. scene v.

> *Our Reasons are not proph|ets,*
> *When oft our Fancies are.*—Act V. scene v.

The hints which you have now perused, are not, I repeat, offered to you as by any means exhausting the elements of Shakspeare's manner of writing. They are meant only to bring to your memory such of his qualities of style as chiefly distinguish him from Fletcher, and are most prominently present in the play we are examining. When we shall see those qualities instanced singly, they will

In bits of the Two Noble Kinsmen several of Shakspere's distinctive qualities are often combin'd.

afford a proof of Shakspeare's authorship : but that proof will receive an incalculable accession of strength when, as will more frequently happen, we shall have several of them displayed at once in the same passages. Your recollection of them will serve us as the lines of a map would in a journey on foot through a wild forest country : the beauty of the landscape will tempt us not seldom to diverge and lose sight of our path, and we shall need their guidance for enabling us to regain it.

The story of Palamon and Arcite.

The story of PALAMON AND ARCITE is a celebrated one, and, besides its appearance here, has been taken up by other two of our greatest English poets. Chaucer borrowed the tale from the *Teseide* of Boccaccio : it then received a dramatic form in this play ; and from Chaucer's antique sketch it was afterwards decorated with the trappings of heroic rhyme, by one who fell on evil days, the lofty and unfortunate Dryden. It treats of a period of ancient and al- Character of the story of Palamon and Arcite. most fabulous history, which originally belonged to the classical writers, but had become familiar in the chivalrous poetry of the middle ages; and retaining the old historical characters, it intersperses with them new ones wholly imaginary, and, both in the Knightes Tale and in the play, preserves the rich and anomalous magnificence of the Gothic cos¹tume. The character round which [¹ page 28] the others are grouped, one which Shakspeare has introduced in Theseus the centre of *The Two Noble Kinsmen.* another of his works, is the heroic Theseus, whom the romances and chronicles dignify with the modern title of Duke of Athens; and in this story he is connected with the tragical war of the Seven against Thebes, one of the grandest subjects of the ancient Grecian poetry.

The whole of the First Act may be safely pronounced to be First Act of *Two Noble Kinsmen* Shakspere's. Shakspeare's. The play opens with the bridal procession of Theseus and the fair Amazon Hippolita, whose young sister EMILIA is the lady of the tale. While the marriage-song is singing, the train are met by three queens in mourning attire, who fall down at the feet of Theseus, Hippolita, and Emilia. They are the widows of three of the princes slain in battle before Thebes, and the conqueror Creon has refused the remains of the dead soldiers the last honour of a grave. The prayer of the unfortunate ladies to Theseus is, that he would raise his powerful arm to force from the tyrant the unburied corpses, that the ghosts of the dead may be appeased by the performance of fitting rites of sepulture. The duty which knighthood imposed on the Prince of Athens, is combated by his unwillingness to quit his bridal happiness; but generosity and self-denial at length obtain the victory, and he marches, with banners displayed, to attack the Thebans.

This scene bears decided marks of Shakspeare.—The lyrical pieces scattered through his plays are, whether successful or not, endowed with a stateliness of rhythm, an originality and clearness of imagery, and a nervous quaintness and pomp of language, which can scarcely be mistaken. The Bridal Song which ushers in this The Bridal Song can't be Fletcher's. play, has several of the marks of distinction, and is very unlike the more formal and polished rhymes of Fletcher.

Act I. sc. i.

The Bridal Song
is Shakspere's.

[¹ page 29]

Primrose, first-born child of Ver,
Merry springtime's harbinger,
   With her bells dim:
Oxlips in their cradles growing,
Marigolds on death-beds blowing,
   Lark-heels trim:
All, dear Nature's children sweet,
Lie 'fore bride and bridegroom's feet,
   ¹*Blessing their sense:*
Not an *angel of the air,*
Bird melodious or bird fair,
   Be absent hence!

Dialogue in I. i.
has the charac-
teristics of
Shakspere's
style:
is crowded,

obscure,

alliterative,

clear and yet
confus'd,

has fulness and
variety,

originality and
true poetry.

But the dialogue which follows is strikingly characteristic. It has sometimes Shakspeare's identical images and words: it has his quaint force and sententious brevity, crowding thoughts and fancies into the narrowest space, and submitting to obscurity in preference to feeble dilation: it has sentiments enunciated with reference to subordinate relations, which other writers would have expressed with less grasp of thought: it has even Shakspeare's alliteration, and one or two of his singularities in conceit: it has clearness in the images taken separately, and confusion from the prodigality with which one is poured out after another, in the heat and hurry of imagination: it has both fulness of illustration, and a variety which is drawn from the most distant sources; and it has, thrown over all, that air of originality and that character of poetry, the principle of which is often hid when their presence and effect are most quickly and in-stinctively perceptible.

    1 *Queen.* (*To Theseus.*) For pity's sake, and true gentility's,
Hear and respect me!
    2 *Queen.* (*To Hippolita.*) For your mother's sake,
And as you wish your womb may thrive with fair | ones,
Hear and respect me!
    3 *Queen.* (*To Emilia.*) Now for the love of him whom Jove
      hath marked
The honour of your bed, and for the sake
Of clear virginity, be advocate
For us and our distresses! This good deed
Shall rase you, out of the Book of Trespasses,
All you are set down there.

These latter lines are of a character which is perfectly and sin- Act I. sc. i.
gularly Shakspeare's. The shade of gravity which so usually dark- Shakspere's gravity and seriousness.
ens his poetry, is often heightened to the most solemn seriousness.
The religious thought presented here is most alien from Fletcher's
turn of thought.—The ensuing speech offers much of Shakspeare.
His energy, sometimes confined within [1] due limits, often betrays him [' page 30] Shakspere sometimes harsh and coarse.
into harshness ; and his liking for familiarity of imagery and expres-
sion sometimes makes him careless though both should be coarse,
a fault which we find here, and of which Fletcher is not guilty.
Here also are more than one of those bold coinages of words, His bold coinages of words :
forced on a mind for whose force of conception common terms
were too weak.

> 1 *Queen.* We are three queens, whose sovrans fell before
> The wrath of cruel Creon ; who endured
> The beaks of ravens, talons of the kites,
> And pecks of crows, in the foul fields of Thebes.
> He will not suffer us to burn their bones,
> To *urn* their ashes, nor to take the offence to *urn* ashes :
> Of mortal loathesomeness from the blest eye
> Of holy Phœbus, but infects the air
> With stench of our slain lords. Oh, pity, Duke !
> Thou purger [1] of the earth ! draw thy fear'd sword,
> That does good turns i' the world : give us the bones
> Of our dead kings, that we may *chapel* them ! to *chapel* bones.
> And, of thy boundless goodness, take some note,
> That for our crowned heads we have no roof
> Save this, which is the lion's and the bear's,
> And vault to every thing.

We now begin to trace more and more that reflecting tendency Shakspere reflective.
which is so deeply imprinted on Shakspeare's writings :—

> *Theseus.*   .   .   .   .
> King Capanëus [2] was your lord : the day
> That he should marry you, at such a seas|on
> As it is now with me, I met your groom
> By Mars's altar. You were that time fair ;

[1] Perhaps it is worth while to direct attention to this form of speech. Ver-
bal names expressing the agent occur, it is true, in Fletcher and others, but they
are in an especial manner frequent with Shakspeare, who invents them to preserve
his brevity, and always applies them with great force and quaintness.

[2] Probably Fletcher would not have committed this false quantity.

Act I. sc. i.

Not Juno's mantle fairer than your tress|es,
Nor in more bounty spread : your wheaten wreath
Was then nor threshed nor blast|ed ' : Fortune, at you,
Dimpled her cheek with smiles : Hercules our kins|man
(Then weaker than your eyes) laid by his club,—
He tumbled down upon his Némean hide,

[page 31]

And swore his sinews thawed. O, Grief and Time,
Fearful consumers, you will all devour !
    1. *Queen.* Oh, I hope some god,
Some god hath put his mercy in your man|hood,
Whereto he'll infuse power, and press you forth,
Our undertaker !
    Theseus.   Oh, no knees ; none, wid|ow !
Unto the helmeted Bellona use | them,
And pray for me, your sol|dier.|—Troubled I am. (*Turns away.*)
    2 *Queen.* Honoured Hippolita, . . .

A Shakspere
fancy.

    .   .   .   dear *glass of la dies !*
Bid him, that we, whom flaming war hath scorch'd,
Under the shadow of his sword may cool us.
Require him, he advance it o'er our heads ;

[3 middle-rymes,
key, three, lance.]

Speak it in a woman's key, like such a wom|an
As any of us three : weep ere you fail ;
Lend us a knee ;—
But touch the ground for us no longer time

A Shakspere
simile.

Than a dove's motion when the head's pluckt off :
Tell him, if he i' the blood-siz'd field lay swol|len,
Shewing the sun his teeth, grinning at the moon,
What you would do !

    .   .   .   .
    Emilia.   Pray stand up ;
Your grief is written on your cheek.
    3 *Queen.*   Oh, woe !
You cannot read it there : there,[1] through my tears, (*'in her eyes*)
Like wrinkled pebbles in a glassy stream,
You may behold it. Lady, lady, alack !
He that will all the treasure know o' the earth,
Must know the centre too : he that will fish

Shakspere.

For my least minnow, let him lead his line
To catch one at my heart. Oh, pardon me !
Extremity, that sharpens sundry wits,
Makes me a fool.
    Emilia.   Pray you, say nothing ; pray | you !
Who cannot feel nor see the rain, being in't,
Knows neither wet nor dry. If that you were
The ground-piece of some painter, I would buy | you,
To instruct me 'gainst a capital grief indeed ;
(Such heart-pierced demonstration ;) but, alas !

Being a natural sister ot our sex,
Your sorrow beats so ardently upon | me,
That it shall make a counter-reflect against
My brother's heart, and warm it to some pit|y,
Though it were made of stone : Pray have good com|fort !

    1 *Queen.* (*To Theseus.*) . . Remember that your fame   [page 32]
Knolls in the ear o' the world : what you do quickl|y,
Is not done rashly ; your first thought, is more
Than others' labour'd meditance ; your premed|itating,
More than their actions : but, (oh, Jove !) your ac|tions,
Soon as they move, *as ospreys do the fish,*   Shakspere
Subdue before they touch. Think, dear duke, think   simile,
What beds our slain kings have !
    2 *Queen.*   What griefs, our beds,
That our slain kings have none.   metaphor.

Theseus is moved by their prayers, but, loth to leave the side of
his newly wedded spouse, contents himself with directing his chief
captain to lead the Athenian army against the tyrant. The queens
redouble their entreaties for his personal aid.

    2 *Queen.* We come unseasonably ; but when could Grief
Cull out, as *unpang'd Judgment* can, fitt'st time   Shakspere
For best solicitation !   personification.
    Theseus.   Why, good la|dies,
This is a service whereto I am go|ing,
Greater than any war : it more imports | me
Than all the actions that I have foregone,
Or futurely can cope.
    1 *Queen.*   The more proclaim|ing
Our suit shall be neglected. When her arms,
Able to lock Jove from a synod, shall
By warranting moonlight *corslet* thee,—oh, when   Shakspere
Her twinning cherries shall their sweetness fall   metaphor,
Upon thy tasteful lips,—what wilt thou think
Of rotten kings or blubberd queens ? what care,
For what thou feel'st not ; what thou feel'st, being a|ble   force.
To make Mars spurn his drum ?—Oh, if thou couch
But one night with her, every hour in't will
Take hostage of thee for a hundred, and
Thou shalt remember nothing more than what
That banquet bids thee to.

    Theseus.   Pray stand up :
I am entreating of myself to do

Act I. sc. i.

That which you kneel to have me.   Perithous !
Lead on the bride !   Get you, and pray the gods
For súccess and return ; omit not any thing
In the pretended celebration.   Queens !
Follow your soldier.   .   .   .   .

[page 33]

    .   .   (*To Hippolita.*) Since that our theme is haste,
I stamp this kiss upon thy currant lip :

Shakspere metaphor.

Sweet, keep it as my token !   .   .   .
  1 *Queen*. Thus dost thou still make good the tongue o' the world.
  2 *Queen*. And earn'st a deity equal with Mars.
  3 *Queen*. If not above him ; for
Thou, being but mortal, mak'st affections bend
To godlike honours ; *they themselves, some say,*

Shakspere.

Groan under such a mas|tery.|
  Theseus.   As we arc men,
Thus should we do : being sensually subdued,
We lose our human title.   Good cheer, la|dies :
Now turn we towards your comforts.   (*Exeu·.t.*)

Act I. scene ii.

The second scene introduces the heroes of the piece, Palamon and Arcite.   They are two youths of the blood-royal of Thebes, who follow the banners of their sovereign with a sense that obedience is their duty, but under a sorrowful conviction that his cause is unjust, and their country rotten at the core.   The scene is a dialogue between them, occupied in lamentations and repinings over the

has the characteristics of Shakspere.

dissolute manners of their native Thebes.   Its broken versification points out Shakspeare ; the quaintness of some conceits is his ; and several of the phrases and images have much of his pointedness, brevity, or obscurity.   The scene, though not lofty in tone, does not want interest, and contains some extremely original illustrations. But quotations will be multiplied abundantly before we have done ; and their number must not be increased by the admission of any which are not either unusually good or very distinctly characteristic of their author.   Some lines of the scene have been already given.

Act I. scene iii.

The third scene has the farewell commendations of the young Emilia and her sister to Perithous, when he sets out to join Theseus, then before the Theban walls, and a subsequent conversation of the

is probably all Shakspere's.

two ladies.   Much of this scene has Shakspeare's stamp deeply cut upon it : it is probably all his.   It is identified, not only by several others of the qualities marking the first scene, but more particularly

by the wealth of its allusion, and by a closeness, directness, and
pertinency of reply which Fletcher's most spirited dialogues do not
reach. It presents more than one exceed¹ingly beautiful climax; a
figure which repeatedly occurs in the play, and is always used with
peculiar energy.

SCENE—*Before the Gates of Athens.—Enter Perithous, Hippolita,*
and Emilia.

  Perithous.   No further.
  Hippolita.   Sir, farewell. Repeat my wish|es
To our great lord, of whose success I dare | not
Make any timorous question ; yet I wish | him
Excess and overflow of power, an't might | be,
To dure ill-dealing Fortune. Speed to him !
Store never hurts good governors.
  Perithous.   Though I know
His ocean needs not my poor drops, yet they
Must yield their tribute there. (*To Emilia.*) My precious maid,
Those best affections that the heavens infuse
In their *best-tempered pieces*, keep *enthroned*   Shakspere
In your dear heart !   metaphor,
  Emilia.   Thanks, sir ! Remember me
To our all-royal brother, for whose speed
The great Bellona I'll solicit ; and,
Since in our terrene state, petitions are | not,
Without gifts, understood, I'll offer to | her
What I shall be advised she likes. Our hearts
Are in his army, in his tent.
  Hippolita.   In's bos|om !
We have been soldiers, and we cannot weep
When our friends dón their helms or put to sea,
Or tell of babes broacht on the lance, or wom'en
That have sod their infants in (and after cat | them)
The brine they wept at killing them ; then if   phrase.
You stay to see of us such spinsters, we
Should hold you here for ever.

  Emilia.   How his long|ing
Follows his friend !
               Have you observëd him
Since our great lord departed ?
  Hippolita.   With much la|bour,
And I did love him for't.²

 ² The remainder of this speech, an extremely fine one, has been quoted incidentally in page 26. Its richness of fancy is wonderful and most characteristic.

Act I. sc. iii.

[¹ page 35]

Female friendship :
the description
has Shakspere's
characteristics.

¹The description of female friendship which follows is familiar to all lovers of poetry. It is disfigured by one or two strained conceits, and some obscurities arising partly from errors in the text : but the beauty of the sketch in many parts is extreme, and its character distinctly that of Shakspeare, vigorous and even quaint, thoughtful and sometimes almost metaphysical, instinct with animation, and pregnant with fancy ; offering, in short, little resmblance to the manner of any poet but Shakspeare, and the most unequivocal opposition to Fletcher's.

    Emilia.   Doubtless
There is a best, and reason has no man|ners
To say, it is not you.   I was acquaint|ed
Once with a time when I enjoy'd a play|fellow——
You were at wars when she the grave enrich'd,
(Who made too proud the bed,) took leave o' the moon,
Which then look'd pale at parting, when our count
Was each eleven.
    Hippolita.   'Twas Flavina.
    Emilia.   Yes.
You talk of Perithous' and Theseus' love :
'Theirs has more ground, is more maturely seas|oned,
More buckled with strong judgment ; and their needs,
The one of the other, may be said to wat,er
Their intertangled roots of love.—But I
And she I sigh and spoke of, were things in|nocent,—
Loved for we did, and,—like the elements,
That know not what nor why, yet do effect
Rare issues by their operance,—our souls
Did so to one another.   What she liked,
Was then of me approved ; what not, condemned.
No more arraign|ment.| The flower that I would pluck,
And put between my breasts, (then but begin|ning
To swell about the blossom,) she would long
Till she had such another, and commit | it
To the like innocent cradle, where, phœnix-like,
They died in perfume ; on my head, no toy
But was her pattern ; her affections, (pret|ty,
Though happily her careless wear,) I fol|low'd
For my most serious decking.—Had mine ear
Stolen some new air, or at adventure humm'd
From musical coinage,—why, it was a note
Whereon her spirits would sojourn, rather dwell | on,
And sing it in her slumbers.—This rehears|al
²(Which, every innocent wots well, comes in

Shakspere fancy.

[² page 36]

Like old importment's bastard) has this end,
That the true love 'tween maid and maid may be
More than in sex dividual.   .   .   .

The fourth scene is laid in a battle-field near Thebes, and Theseus enters victorious. The three queens fall down with thanks before him ; and a herald announces the capture of the Two Noble Kinsmen, wounded and senseless, and scarcely retaining the semblance of life. The phraseology of this short scene is like Shakspeare's, being brief and energetic, and in one or two instances passing into quibbles.

Act I. scene iv. Shakspere's.

Has Shakspere's words and quibbles.

The last scene of this act is of a lyrical cast, and comprised in a few lamentations spoken by the widowed queens over the corpses of their dead lords. It ends with this couplet :

Act I. scene v. is Shakspere's.

The world's a city full of straying streets,
And death's the market-place, where each one meets.

In the Second Act no part seems to have been taken by Shakspeare. It commences with one of those scenes which are introduced into the play in departure from the narrative of Chaucer, forming an underplot which is clearly the work of a different artist from many of the leading parts of the drama. The Noble Kinsmen, cured of their wounds, have been committed to strait and perpetual prison in Athens, and the first part of this scene is a prose dialogue between their jailor and a suitor of his daughter. The maiden's admiration of the prisoners is then exhibited. You will see afterwards, that there are several circumstances besides the essential dulness of this prose part, which fully absolve Shakspeare from the charge of having written it.

Act II. not Shakspere's. The prose of II. i. is not from Chaucer,

and is very dull ; it is not Shakspere's.

The versified portion of this scene, which follows the prose dialogue among the inferior characters, presents the incident on which the interest of the story hinges, the commencement of the fatal and chimerical passion, which, inspiring both the knights towards the young Emilia, severs the bonds of friendship which had so long held them together. The noble prisoners are discovered in their turret-chamber, looking out on the palace-garden, which the lady afterwards enters. They speak [1] in a highly animated strain of that

The verse of Act II. scene i.

[¹ page 37]

world from which they are secluded, and find themes of consolation for the hard lot which had overtaken them. The dialogue is in many respects admirable. It possesses much eloquence of description, and the character of the language is smooth and flowing; the versification is good and accurate, frequent in double endings, and usually finishing the sense with the line; and one or two allusions occur, which, being favourites of Fletcher's, may be in themselves a strong presumption of his authorship; the images too have in some instances a want of distinctness in application or a vagueness of outline, which could be easily paralleled from Fletcher's acknowledged writings. The style is fuller of allusions than his usually is, but the images are more correct and better kept from confusion than Shakspeare's; some of them indeed are exquisite, but rather in the romantic and exclusively poetical tone of Fletcher, than in the natural and universal mode of feeling which animates Shakspeare. The dialogue too proceeds less energetically than Shakspeare's, falling occasionally into a style of long-drawn disquisition which Fletcher often substitutes for the quick and dramatic conversations of the great poet. On the whole, however, this scene, if it be Fletcher's, (of which I have no doubt,) is among the very finest he ever wrote; and there are many passages in which, while he preserves his own distinctive marks, he has gathered no small portion of the flame and inspiration of his immortal friend and assistant. In the following speeches there are images and phrases, which are either identically Fletcher's, or closely resemble his, and the whole cast both of versification and idiom is strictly his :—

The verse of Act II. scene i. has the characteristics of Fletcher:

double endings,

end-stopt lines,

vague images,

but romantic;

slack dialogue.

II. i. one of the finest scenes that Fletcher ever wrote.

> *Palamon.*   Oh, cousin Ar|cite !
> Where is Thebes now? where is our noble coun|try?
> Where are our friends and kindreds?   Never more
> Must we behold those comforts; never see
> The hardy youths strive in the games of hon|our,
> Hung with the painted favours of their la|dies,
> Like tall ships under sail; then start among | them,
> And as an east wind leave them all behind | us
> Like lazy clouds, while Palamon and Ar|cite,
> Even in the wagging of a wanton leg,
> Outstript the people's praises, won the gar|lands,

Ere they have time to wish them ours.   Oh, nev|er
Shall we two exercise, like twins of hon|our,
Our arms again, and feel our fiery hors|es
Like proud seas under us ! our good swords now,
(Better the red-eyed god of war ne'er wore,)
Ravish'd our sides, like age must run to rust,
And deck the temples of the gods that hate | us :
These hands shall never draw them out like light|ning
To blast whole armies more.

   Arcite.   .   .   .   .

The sweet embraces of a loving wife,
Loaden with kisses, arm'd with thousand cu|pids,
Shall never clasp our necks : no issue know | us ;
No figures of ourselves shall we e'er see,
To glad our age, and like young eagles teach | them
Boldly to gaze against bright arms, and say,
" Remember what your fathers were, and con|quer."
—The fair-eyed maids shall weep our banishments,
And in their songs curse ever-blinded For|tune,
Till she for shame see what a wrong she has done
To youth and Nature.—This is all our world :—
We shall know nothing here but one anoth|er,—
Hear nothing but the clock that tells our woes ;
The vine shall grow, but we shall never see | it :
Summer shall come, and with her all delights,
But dead-cold winter must inhabit here | still !

   Palamon. 'Tis too true, Arcite ! To our Theban hounds,
That shook the aged forest with their ech|oes,
No more now must we halloo ; no more shake
Our pointed javelins, whilst the angry swine
Flies like a Parthian [1] quiver from our rag|es,
Struck with our well-steel'd darts.   .

In this scene there is one train of metaphors which is perhaps as characteristic of Fletcher as any thing that could be produced.   It is marked by a slowness of association which he often shews. Several allusions are successively introduced ; but by each, as it appears, we are prepared for and can anticipate the next ; we see the connection of ideas in the poet's mind through which the one has sprung out of the other, and that all are but branches, of which one original thought is the root.   All this is the work of [2] a less

---

[1] This allusion is repeatedly found in Fletcher.   Here the expression of it is defective in precision.

Marginal notes:

[page 38]
Act II. scene i.
Fletcher's.

Picture ful'y
wrought out.

Romantic,
pathetic sketch.

Lines from II. i.
on page 38, of
slow orderly
development of
ideas, markt by
Fletcher's
characteristics.

[² page 39]

Act II. scene i.
No leap to the
end, and off with
a fresh bound,
like Shakspere.

fertile fancy and a more tardy understanding than Shakspeare's : he would have leaped over many of the intervening steps, and, reaching at once the most remote particular of the series, would have immediately turned away to weave some new chain of thought :—

> *Arcite.*   .   .   .   What worthy bless|ing
> Can be, but our imaginatiöns
> May make it ours ? and here, being thus togeth|er,
> We are an endless mine to one anoth|er :
> We are one another's wife, ever beget|ting
> New births of love ; we are fathers, friends, acquaint|ance ;
> We are, in one another, families ;
> I am your heir and you are mine ; this place
> Is our inheritance ; no hard oppress|or
> Dare take this from us.   .   .   .

All workt out
thro' every step.

But the contentment of the prison is to be interrupted. The fair Emilia appears beneath, walking in the garden "full of branches green," skirting the wall of the tower in which the princes are confined. She converses with her attendant, and Palamon from the dungeon-grating beholds her as she gathers the flowers of spring. He ceases to reply to Arcite, and stands absorbed in silent ecstasy.

> *Arcite.* Cousin ! How do you, sir? Why, Palamon !
> *Palamon.* Never till now I was in prison, Ar|cite.
> *Arcite.* Why, what's the matter, man ?
> *Palamon.*   Behold and won|der :
> By heaven, she is a goddess ;
> *Arcite.*   Ha !
> *Palamon.*   Do rev|erence ;
> She is a goddess, Arcite !

The sharp and
spirited quarrel
between the
Kinsmen, not
Shakspere's.

The beauty of the maiden impresses Arcite no less violently than it previously had his kinsman ; and he challenges with great heat a right to love her. An animated and acrimonious dialogue ensues, in which Palamon reproachfully pleads his prior admiration of the lady, and insists on his cousin's obligation to become his abettor instead of his rival. It is spirited even to excess ; and probably Shakspeare would have tempered, or abstained from treating so sudden and perhaps unnatural an access of anger and jealousy, [1 page 40] and so utter an abandonment to [1]its vehemence, as that under which the fiery Palamon is here represented as labouring.

Palamon.   If thou lovest her,
Or entertain'st a hope to blast my wish|es,
Thou art a traitor, Arcite, and a fellow
False as thy title to her.   Friendship, blood,
And all the ties between us, I disclaim,
If thou once think upon her !
    Arcite.   Yes, I love | her !
And, if the lives of all my name lay on | it,
I must do so.   I love her with my soul ;
If that will lose thee, Palamon, farewell !
I say again I love, and, loving her
I am as worthy and as free a lov|er,
And have as just a title to her beau|ty,
As any Palamon, or any liv|ing
That is a man's son !
    Palamon.   Have I call'd thee friend !

.   .   .

Palamon. Put but thy head out of this window more,
And, as I have a soul, I'll nail thy life to't !
    Arcite. Thou dar'st not, fool : thou canst not : thou art fee|ble :
Put my head out ? I'll throw my body out,
And leap the garden, when I see her next,
And pitch between her arms to anger thee.

Act II. scene i.
Fletcher's

In transferring his story from Chaucer, the poet has here been
guilty of an oversight.   The old poet fixes a character of positive
guilt on Arcite's prosecution of his passion, by relating a previous
agreement between the two cousins, by which either, engaging in
any adventure whether of love or war, had an express right to the
co-operation of the other.   Hence Arcite's interference with his
cousin's claim becomes, with Chaucer, a direct infringement of a
knightly compact ; while in the drama, no deeper blame attaches to
it, than as a violation of the more fragile rules imposed by the
generous spirit of friendship.

Fletcher has left
out Chaucer's
making the
Knights ' sworn
brethren.'

In the midst of the angry conference, Arcite is called to the Duke
to receive his freedom ; and Palamon is placed in stricter confine-
ment, and removed from the quarter of the tower overlooking the
garden.

In the second scene of this act, Arcite, wandering in the [1]neigh-
bourhood of Athens, soliloquizes on the decree which had banished
him from the Athenian territory ; and, falling in with a band of
country people on their way to games in the city, conceives the

Act II. scene ii.
(Weber, sc. iii,
Littledale)
is Fletcher's.
[¹ page 41]

notion of joining in the celebration under some poor disguise, in the hope of finding means to remain within .sight of his fancifully be-

Act II. scene ii.
iii. (Weber, sc.
iii. iv. Little-
dale),

loved mistress. Neither this scene, nor the following, in which the jailor's daughter meditates on the perfections of Palamon, and inti-mates an intention of assisting him to escape, have any thing in them worthy of particular notice.

Act II. scene iv.
(Weber, sc. v.
Littledale),

In the fourth scene, Arcite, victorious in the athletic games, is crowned by the Duke, and preferred to the service of Emilia.

Act II. scene v.
(Weber, sc. vi.
(Littledale),
are all Fletcher's.

In the last scene of the second act, the jailor's daughter an-nounces that she has effected Palamon's deliverance from prison, and that he lies hidden in a wood near the city, the scenery of which is prettily described.

Act III. scene i.
is Shakspere's.

Nothing in the Third Act can with confidence be attributed to Shakspeare, except the first scene. This opening scene is laid in the wood where Palamon has his hiding-place. Arcite enters; and a monologue, describing his situation and feelings, is, as in Chaucer, overheard by Palamon, who starts out of the bush in which he had crouched, and shakes his fettered hands at his false kinsman. A dialogue of mutual reproach ensues; and Arcite departs with a pro-mise to return, bringing food for the outcast, and armour to fit him

Arcite's first
speech has
Shakspere's clear
images, and
familiar dress,
nervous
expression, &c.

for maintaining, like a knight, his right to the lady's love. The commencing speech of Arcite has much of Shakspeare's clearness of imagery, and of the familiarity of dress which he often loves to bestow upon allusion; it has also great nerve of expression and calm-ness of tone, with at least one play on words which is quite in his manner, and one (perhaps more) of his identical phrases. The text seems faulty in one part.

> *Arcite.* The Duke has lost Hippolita : each took
> A several laund.   This is a solemn rite
> They owe bloom'd May, and the Athenians pay it
> *To the heart of ceremony.*   Oh, queen Emillia !
> Fresher than May, sweeter
> Than her *gold buttons* on the boughs, or all
> The enamell'd knacks o' the mead or garden !   Yea,
> We challenge too the bank of any nymph,
> That makes the stream seem flowers !—Thou,—oh jewel

Shaksperean
phrases.

[page 42]

O' the wood, o' the world,—hast likewise blest a place
With thy sole presence. In thy rumina|tion
That I, poor man, might eftsoons come between,
And chop on some cold thought !—Thrice blessed chance,
To drop on such a mistress !   Expecta|tion
Most guiltless of | it.| Tell me, oh lady For tune,
(Next after Emily my sovran,) how far
I may be proud. She takes strong note of me,
Hath made me near her, and this beauteous morn,
(The primest of all the year,) presents me with
A brace of horses ; two such steeds might well
· Be by a pair of kings back'd, in a field
That their crowns' titles tried. Alas, alas !
Poor cousin Palamon, poor prisoner !   ·

·   ·   ·   ·   If
Thou knew'st my mistress breathed on me, and that
I *eared* her language, lived in her eye, oh coz,
What passion would enclose thee !

Act III. sc. i. is
Shakspere's.

Shakspere
phrase.

There is great spirit, also, in what follows. Some phrases, here
again, are precisely Shakspeare's ; and several parts of the dialogue
have much of his pointed epigrammatic style. The massive ac-
cumulation of reproaches which Palamon hurls on Arcite is, in its
energy, more like him than his assistant; and the opposition of
character between Palamon and his calmer kinsman, is well kept
up ; but the dialogue cannot be accounted one of the best in the
play.

  Palamon. · · Oh, thou most perfid|ious
That ever gently look'd !   The void'st of hon|our
That e'er bore gentle token !   Falsest cous|in
That ever blood made kin ! call'st thou her thine ?
I'll prove it in my shackles, in these hands
Void of appointment, that thou liest, and art
A very thief in love, a chaffy lord,
Not worth the name of villain !—Had I a sword,
And these house-clogs away !
  Arcite.   *Dear cousin Pal|amon !*
  Palamon. Cozener Arcite ! give me language such
As thou hast shewed me feat.
  Arcite.   Not finding in
The circuit of my breast, any gross stuff
To form me like your *blazon*, holds me to
This gentleness of answer. 'Tis your pas|sion
That thus mistakes ; the which, to you being en|emy,
Cannot to me be kind. · · ·

Shaksperean
string of epithets.

Shaksperean
word-play.

[page 43]

Act III. scene ii.   In the second scene, the only speaker is the jailor's daughter, who, having lost Palamon in the wood, begins to shew symptoms of unsettled reason.   There is some pathos in several parts of her soliloquy, but little vigour in the expression, or novelty in the thoughts.

Act III. scene iii.   The third scene is an exchange of brief speeches between the two knights.   Arcite brings provisions for his kinsman, and the means of removing his fetters, and departs to fetch the armour.   In

is probably Fletcher's,   most respects the scene is not very characteristic of either writer, but leans towards Fletcher ; and one argument for him might be drawn from an interchange of sarcasms between the kinsmen, in which they retort on each other, former amorous adventures : such a dialogue is quite like Fletcher's men of gaiety ; and needless degrada-

and not Shakspere's.   tion of his principal characters, is a fault of which Shakspeare is not guilty.   You may be able, hereafter, to see more distinctly the force of this reason.   The scene contains one strikingly animated burst of jealous suspicion and impatience.

> *Arcite.* Pray you sit down then ; and let me entreat | you,
> By all the honesty and honour in | you,
> No mention of this woman ; 'twill disturb | us ;
> We shall have time enough.
> *Palamon.*   Well, sir, I'll pledge | you.
>
> *Arcite.* Heigh-ho !
> *Palamon.*   For Emily, upon my life !—Fool,
> Away with this strained mirth !—I say again,
> That sigh was breathed for Emily.   Base cous|in,
> Darest thou break first ?
> *Arcite.*   You are wide.
> *Palamon.*   By heaven and earth,
> There's nothing in thee honest !

Act III. scenes iv. v.   [¹ page 44]   In the next two scenes, placed in the forest, the jailor's daughter has reached the height of frenzy.   She meets the country¹men who had encountered Arcite, and who are now headed by the learned

Gerrold has no spark of humour.   and high-fantastical schoolmaster Gerrold, a personage who has the pedantry of Shakspeare's Holofernes, without one solitary spark of his humour.   They are preparing a dance for the presence of the duke, and the maniac is adopted into their number, to fill up a vacancy.   The duke and his train appear,—the pedagogue prologuizes,

—the clowns dance,—and their self-satisfied Coryphaeus apologizes and epiloguizes. Some of Fletcher's very phrases and forms of expression have been traced in these two scenes.

We have then, in the sixth and last scene of this act, the inter- rupted combat of the two princes. The scene is a spirited and excellent one ; but its tone is Fletcher's, not Shakspeare's. The rail- lery and retort of the dialogue is more lightly playful than his, and less antithetical and sententious ; and though there are fine images, they are not seized with the grasp which Shakspeare would have given, sometimes harsh, but always at least decided. Some of the illustrations have been quoted (page 17). The knightly courtesy with which the princes arm each other is well supported ; and their dignity of greeting before they cross their swords, is fine, exceedingly fine. Nothing can be more beautifully conceived than the change which comes over the temper of the generous Palamon, when he stands on the verge of mortal battle with his enemy. His usual heat and impatience give place to the most becoming calmness. The versification is very sweet, and the romantic air of the phrase- ology is very much Fletcher's, especially towards the end of the following quotation.

> *Palamon.*　　　　My cause and honour guard | me.
> (*They bow several ways, then advance and stand.*)
> *Arcite.* And me my love ; Is there aught else to say ?
> *Palamon.* This only, and no more : Thou art mine aunt's | son,
> And that blood we desire to shed is mu|tual ;
> In me, thine ; and in thee, mine. My sword
> Is in my hand, and, if thou killest me,
> The gods and I forgive thee ! If there .be
> A place prepared for those that sleep in hon|our,
> I wish his weary soul that falls may win | it !
> Fight bravely, cous|in ;| give me thy noble hand !
> *Arcite.* Here, Palamon : this hand shall never more　　　[page 45]
> Come near thee with such friendship.
> *Palamon.*　　　　　　　　I commend | thee.
> *Arcite.* If I fall, curse me, and say I was a cow|ard ;
> For none but such dare die in these just tri|als.
> Once more farewell, my cousin.
> *Palamon.*　　　　　　Farewell, Ar|cite.
> 　　　　　　　　　　(*They fight.*)

The combat is interrupted by the approach of the Duke and his

Act III. scene vi.

court; and Palamon, refusing to give back or conceal himself, appears before Theseus, and declares his own name and situation, and the presumptuous secret of Arcite. The scene is good, but in the flowing style of Fletcher, not the more manly one of Shakspeare. The sentence of death, which the duke, in the first moments of his anger, pronounces on the two princes, is recalled on the petition of Hippolita and her sister, on condition that the rivals shall meantime depart, and return within a month, each accompanied by three knights, to determine in combat the possession of Emilia; and death by the block is denounced against the knights who shall be vanquished. Some of these circumstances are slight deviations from Chaucer; and the laying down of the severe penalty is well imagined, as an addition to the tragic interest, giving occasion to a very impressive scene in the last act.

is in Fletcher's style.

Death-penalty for the losing knight, a good addition to Chaucer.

Act IV. all Fletcher's.

Wants all the leading features of Shakspere's style.

The Fourth Act may safely be pronounced wholly Fletcher's. All of it, except one scene, is taken up by the episodical adventures of the jailor's daughter; and, while much of it is poetical, it wants the force and originality, and, indeed, all the prominent features of Shakspeare's manner, either of thought, illustration, or expression. There are conversations in which are described, pleasingly enough, the madness of the unfortunate girl, and the finding of her in a sylvan spot, by her former wooer; but when the maniac herself appears, the tone and subjects of the dialogue become more objectionable.

Act IV. scene ii.

[¹ page 46]

Emilia's soliloquy on the pictures, not Shakspere's.

In the second scene of this act, the only one which bears reference to the main business of the piece, Emilia first muses over the pictures of her two suitors, and then hears from a messenger, in presence of Theseus and his attendants, a description, (taken in ¹its elements from the Knightes Tale,) of the warriors who were preparing for the field along with the champion lovers. In the soliloquy of the lady, while the poetical spirit is well preserved, the alternations of feeling are given with an abruptness and a want of insight into the nicer shades of association, which resemble the extravagant stage effects of the 'King and No King,' infinitely more than the delicate yet piercing glance with which Shakspeare looks into the human breast in the 'Othello'; the language, too, is smoother and less powerful than Shakspeare's, and one or two classical allusions are a little too correct and studied for him. One image occurs, not the clearest or most chastened, in which Fletcher closely repeats himself :—

What a brow,
Of what a spacious majesty, he car|ries !
Arched like the great-eyed Juno's, but far sweet|er,—
Smoother than Pelop's shoulder. Fame and Hon our,
Methinks, from hence, as from a promontor|y
Pointed in Heaven, should clap their wings, and sing
To all the under-world, the loves and fights
Of gods and such men near them.[1]

Act IV. scene ii. Fletcher's.

His description of Arcite, paralleld in his Philaster.

In the Fifth Act we again feel the presence of the Master of the Spell. Several passages in this portion are marked by as striking tokens of his art as anything which we read in ' Macbeth ' or ' Coriolanus.' The whole act, a very long one, may be boldly attributed to him, with the exception of one episodical scene.

Act V. is Shakspere's,

The time has arrived for the combat. Three temples are exhibited, as in Chaucer, in which the rival Knights, and the [1]Lady of their Vows, respectively pay their adorations. One principal aim of their supplications is to learn the result of the coming contest; but the suspense is kept up by each of the Knights receiving a favourable response, and Emilia a doubtful one. Three scenes are thus occupied, the second of which is in somewhat a lower key than the other two; but even in it there is much beauty; and in the first and third the tense dignity and pointedness of the language, the gorgeousness and overflow of illustration, and the reach, the mingled familiarity and elevation of thought, are admirable, inimitable, and decisive.

except scene iv. (Weber: sc. ii. Littledale).
[² page 47]'

Act V. sc. ii. (i. L.) is lower in key.
Act V. sc. i. iii. (Weber: both i. Littledale) are Shakspere's all through.

[1] In Philaster, Act IV. last scene.

Place me, some god, upon a Piramis,
Higher than hill of earth, and lend a voice,
Loud as your thunder, to me, that from thence
I may discourse, to all the under world,
The worth that dwells in him.

Shakspeare, too, was not the most likely person to have given the true meaning of the βοωπις ποτνια 'Ηρη. I am not aware that either Hall or Chapman shewed him the way. Chapman in the First Book (v. 551) has it ; " She with the cowes fair eyes, Respected Juno."

[² 2 *N. K.*, Act V. sc. i, ii, iii. Weber, are V. i. Littledale.]

From these exquisite scenes there is a temptation to quote too largely.

In the first scene, Theseus ushers the Kinsmen and their Knights into the Temple of Mars, and leaves them there. After a short and solemn greeting, the Kinsmen embrace for the last time, Palamon and his friends retire, and Arcite and his remain and offer up their

devotions to the deity of the place. A fine seriousness of spirit breathes through the whole scene, and the language is alive with the most magnificent and delicate allusion. In Arcite's prayer the tone cannot be mistaken. The enumeration of the god's attributes is

coloured by all that energetic depth of feeling with which Shakspeare in his historical dramas so often turns aside to meditate on the changes of human fortune and the horrors of human enmity.[1]

> *Theseus.* You valiant and strong-hearted enemies,
> You royal germane foes, that this day come
> To blow the nearness out that flames between | ye,—
> Lay by your anger for an hour, and dove|-like,
> Before the holy altars of your Help|ers
> (The all-feard Gods) bow down your stubborn bod ies :
> Your ire is more than mortal : so your help | be !

> *Arcite.*   .   .   .   Hoist | we
> Those sails that must these vessels port even where
> The Heavenly Limiter pleases !

> Knights, kinsmen, lovers, yea, my sacrifi|ces !
> True worshippers of Mars, whose spirit in you
> Expels the seeds of fear, and the apprehen|sion
> Which still is father of it,—go with me
> Before the god of our profession. There
> Require of him the hearts of lions, and
> *The breath of tigers, yea the fierceness too,*
> *Yea the speed also !* to go on I mean,
> Else wish we to be snails. You know my prize
> Must be draggd out of blood : Force and great Feat
> Must put my garland on, where she will stick
> The queen of flowers ; our intercession then
> Must be to him that makes the camp *a ces|tron*
> *Brimmd with the blood of men :* give me your aid,
> And bend your spirits towards him !

---

[1] This beautiful address has been spoken of already.

(They fall prostrate before the statue.)

Thou mighty one ! that with thy power has turn'd
Green Neptune into purple,—whose approach
Comets prewarn,—*whose havock in vast field*
Unearthèd skulls proclaim,—whose breath blows down
The teeming Ceres' foyson,—who dost pluck
With hand armipotent from forth blue clouds
The masoned turrets,—that both mak'st and break'st
The stony girths of cities ;—me, thy pup|il,
Young'st follower of thy drum, instruct this day
With military skill, that to thy laud
I may advance my streamer, and by thee
Be styled the lord o' the day : Give me, great Mars,
Some token of thy pleasure !

*(Here there is heard clanging of armour, with a short
thunder, as the burst of a battle ; whereupon they all
rise and bow to the altar.)*

Oh, great Corrector of enormous times !
Shaker of o'er-rank states ! Thou grand Decid|er
Of dusty and old ti|tles ;|—*that heal'st with blood*
The earth when it is sick, and cur'st the world
O' the pleurisy of people ! I do take
Thy signs auspiciously, and in thy name
To my design march boldly.   Let us go !   *(Exeunt.)*

The passionate and sensitive Palamon has chosen the Queen of
Love as his Patroness, and it is in her Temple that, in the [1]second
scene, he puts up his prayers. This scene is not equal to the first
or third, having the poetical features less prominently brought out,
while the tone of thought is less highly pitched, and also less consistently sustained. But it is distinctly Shakspeare's. The rugged
versification is his, and the force of language.   One unpleasing
sketch of the deformity of decrepit old age, which need not be
quoted, is largely impressed with his air of truth, and some personifications already noticed are also in his manner.

Palamon's prayer
in V. ii. (i. L.) not
equal to V. i. or
iii. (i. L.), but
is yet clearly
Shakspere's.
[¹ page 49]

Even the incom-
petent old
husband bit is his.

Palamon. Our stars must glister with new fire, or be
To-day extinct : our argument is love !
.   .   .   *(They kneel.)*
Hail, sovereign Queen of Secrets ! who hast pow|er
To call the fiercest tyrant from his rage
To weep unto a girl !—that hast the might

Even with an eye-glance to choke Mars's drum,
And turn the alarm to whis|pers !| .   .
                      What gold-like pow|er
Hast thou not power upon ? To Phœbus thou
Add'st flames hotter than his : the heavenly fires
Did scorch his mortal son, thou him : The Hunt'ress
All moist and cold, some say, began to throw
Her bow away and sigh.   Take to thy grace
Me thy vowd soldier,—who do bear thy yoke
As 'twere a wreath of roses, yet is heav|ier
Than lead itself, stings more than net|tles :—
I have never been foul-mouthed against thy law ;
            .   .   I have been harsh
To large confessors, and have hotly askt | them
If they had mothers : *I* had one,—a wom|an,
And women 'twere they wronged.   .   .
        .   .   .   Brief,—I am
To those that prate and have done,—no compan|ion ;
To those that boast and have not,—a defi|er ;
To those that would and cannot,—a rejoi|cer !
Yea, him I do not love, that tells close offices
The foulest way, nor names concealments in
The boldest language : Such a one I am,
And vow that *lover never yet made sigh*

Truer than I.   .   .   .   .

(*Music is heard, and doves are seen to flutter : they fall
upon their faces.*)

                  .   I give thee thanks
For this fair token !   .   .   .

Emilia's Prayer in the Sanctuary of the pure Diana, forming
the third scene, is in some parts most nervous, and the opening is
inexpressibly beautiful in language and rhythm.   Several ideas and
idioms are identically Shakspeare's.

Emilia. (*Kneeling before the altar.*) Oh, sacred, shadowy, cold,
            and constant Queen !
Abandoner of revels ! mute, contemplative,
Sweet, solitary, white as chaste, and pure
As wind-fanned snow !—who to thy *female knights*
Allow'st no more blood than will make a blush,
Which is there order's robe !—I here, thy priest,
Am humbled 'fore thine altar. Oh, vouchsafe,

With that thy rare *green eye*,[1] which never yet
Beheld thing maculate, look on thy virg|in !
And,—sacred silver Mistress !—lend thine ear,
(Which ne'er heard scurril term, into whose port
Ne'er entered wanton sound,) to my petit,ion
Seasoned with holy fear !—This is my last
Of vestal office : [2]I'm bride-habited,
But maiden-heart|ed.| A husband I have, appoint|ed,
But do not know him : out of two I should
Chuse one, and pray for his success, but I
Am guiltless of election of mine eyes.[2]

. . . . . .

*(A rose-tree ascends from under the altar, having one rose
upon it.)*

See what our general of ebbs and flows
Out from the bowels of her holy al|tar
With sacred act advances ! But one rose ?
If well inspired, this battle shall confound
Both these brave knights, and I a virgin flow|er
Must grow alone unplucked.

*(Here is heard a sudden twang of instruments, and the rose
falls from the tree.)*

The flower is fallen, the tree descends !—oh, mis|tress,
Thou here dischargest me : I shall be gath|ered,
I think so ; but I know not thine own will ;
Unclasp thy mystery !—I hope she's pleased ;
Her signs were gracious. (*Exeunt.*)

The fourth scene, in which the characters are the jailor's
daughter, her father and lover, and a physician, is disgusting and
imbecile in the extreme. It may be dismissed with a single quotation :

Doctor. What stuff she utters !

The fifth scene is the Combat, the arrangement of which is unusual. Perhaps there is nothing in every respect resembling it in the
circle of the English drama. Theseus and his court cross the stage
as proceeding to the lists ; Emilia pauses and refuses to be present ;
the rest depart, and she is left. She then, the prize of the struggle,

Side notes:

Act V. scene iii.
(Weber ; i.
Littledale)
Shakspere's.

[2—2 This is the
character of
Emilia, by
Chaucer and
Shakspere, but
not by Fletcher of
IV. ii., and the
author of V. v.
(or iii. Littledale)
—if he is not
Fletcher—
with their incon-
sistencies of
Emilia's weak
balancing of
Palamon against
Arcite, now
liking one best,
then the other,
and being afraid
that Palamon
may get his
figure spoilt !
F. J. F.]

[page 51]

Act V. scene iv.
(Weber ; ii.
Littledale)
is stuff.

Act V. scene v.
(Weber ; iii.
Littledale).
Its strangeness.

✱

---

[1] Romeo and Juliet :—Midsummer Night's Dream :—also in Don Quixote,
Parte II. capit. xi. : " Los ojos de Dulcinea deben ser de *verdes esmeraldas.*"

Act V. scene v.
(Weber, or sc. iii.
Littledale).
the presiding influence of the day, alone occupies the stage : within, the trumpets are heard sounding the charge, and the cries of the spectators and tumult of the encounter reach her ears ; one or two messengers recount to her the various changes of the field, till Arcite's victory ends the fight.   The manner is admirable in which the caution, which rendered it advisable to avoid introducing the combat on the stage, is reconciled with the pomp of scenic effect and bustle.   The details of the scene, with which alone we have here to
Shakspere's hand is in it. do, make it clear that Shakspeare's hand was in it.   The greater part, it is true, is not of the highest excellence ; but the vacillations of Emilia's feelings are well and delicately given, some individual thoughts and words mark Shakspeare, there is a little of his obscure brevity, much of his thoughtfulness legitimately applied, and an instance or two of its abuse.   The strong likeness to him will justify some quotations.

In the following lines Theseus is pleading with Emilia for her presence in the lists :—

> *Theseus.*   You must be there :
> This trial is as 'twere in the night, and you
> The only star to shine.
> *Emilia.*   I am extinct.
> There is but envy in that light, which shews
> The one the other.   Darkness, which ever was
> The dam of Horror, who does stand accursed
> Of many mortal millions, may even now,
> By casting her black mantle over both
> That neither could find other, get herself
> Some part of a good name, and many a mur|der
> Set off whereto she's guilty.[1]

Shakspere.

[page 52]

Shakspere.

.   .   .   .

One good description is put into the mouth of Emilia after she is left alone :—

> *Emilia.* Arcite is gently visaged ; yet his eye
> Is like an engine bent, or a sharp weap|on
> In a soft sheath : Mercy and manly Cour|age
> Are bedfellows in his visage.   Palamon

---

[1] The thought here is frequent in Shakspeare's dramas: and the expression of it closely resembles some stanzas in the Lucrece, especially those beginning, "Oh, comfort-killing night ! "

Has a most menacing aspect: his brow
Is graved, and seems to bury what it frowns | on ;
Yet sometimes 'tis not so, but alters to
The quality of his thoughts : long time his eye
Will dwell upon his object : melancholly
Becomes him nobly ; so does Arcite's mirth :
But Palamon's sadness is a kind of mirth,
So mingled, as if mirth did make him sad,
And sadness mer|ry :| those darker humours that
Stick unbecomingly on oth|ers,| on him
Live in fair dwelling.

*Act V. scene v.
(Weber ; or sc.
iii. Littledale).
Shakspere's hand
in it.*

Shakspere.

After several alternations of fortune in the fight, she again speaks
thus of the two :

    ·   ·   ·   Were they metamor phosed
Both into one—oh why ? there were no wom,an
Worth so composed a man ! their single share,
Their nobleness peculiar to them, gives
The prejudice of dispar;ity,| value's shortness,
To any lady breathing.   ·   ·   ·   ·
  (*Cornets : a great shout, and cry,* Arcite, victory !)
  Servant.   The cry is
Arcite and victory ! Hark, Arcite, vic|tory !
The combat's consummation is proclaimed
By the wind instruments.
  Emilia.   Half-sights saw
That Arcite was no babe : god's-lid ! *his rich|ness
And costliness of spirit looked through | him :* | it could
No more be hid in him than fire in flax,
Than humble banks can go to law with wa|ters
That drift winds force to raging. I did think
Good Palamon would miscarry ; yet I knew | not
Why I did think | so.| *Our Reasons are not proph|ets
When oft our Fancies are.* They're coming off :
Alas, poor Palamon !

*(Cp. Beatrice on
Don John and
Benedick, in
Much Ado, II. i.)*

[page 53]

Shakspere touch.

*Shakspere
reflection.*

Theseus enters with his attendants, conducting Arcite, as conqueror, and presents him to Emilia as her husband. Arcite's situation is a painful one, and is well discriminated : he utters but a
single grave sentence.

    Theseus. (*To Arcite and Emilia.*) Give me your hands :
  Receive you her, you him : be plighted with
  A love that grows as you decay !

Act V. scene v.
(Weber; or iii.
Littledale).

Arcite.   Emily !
To buy you I have lost what's dearest to | me,
Save what is bought ; and yet I purchase cheap ly,
As I do rate your value.

.   .   .   .   .   .

Theseus. (*To Arcite.*)   Wear the gar|land
With joy that you have won.   For the subdued,—

Shakspere touch.

Give them our present justice, *since I know*
Their lives but pinch them. Let it here be done.
The sight's not for our seeing : go we hence
Right joyful, with some sorrow !—Arm your prize :
I know you will not lose | her.| Hippolita,
I see one eye of yours conceives a tear,
The which it will deliv|er.|
     Emilia.   Is this, winning?
Oh, all you heavenly powers ! where is your mer|cy ?
But that your wills have said it must be so,
And charge me live to comfort this unfriend|ed,
This miserable prince, that cuts away
A life more worthy from him than all wom|en,
I should and would die too.

[page 54]

     Hippolita.   Infinite pity,
That four such eyes should be so fixed on one,
That two must needs be blind for't.   (*Exeunt.*)

Act V. scene vi.
(Weber ; sc. iv.
Littledale)
is clearly Shak-
spere's.

The authorship of the last scene admits of no doubt. The manner is Shakspeare's, and some parts are little inferior to his very finest passages. Palamon has been vanquished, and he and his friends are to undergo execution of the sentence to which the laws of the combat subjected them. The depth of the interest is now fixed on these unfortunate knights, and a fine spirit of resigned melancholy inspires the scene in which they pass to their deaths.[1]

---

[1] It may be well to mention, that this scene contains allusions, extending through several lines, to the every-way luckless jailor's daughter. If I conceal the fact from you, you will, on finding it out for yourself, suspect that I consider it as making against my hypothesis, which assigns those episodical adventures to a different author from this scene. Be assured that I do not regard it in that light. It is plain that the underplot, however bad, has been worked up with much pains ; and we can conceive that its author would have been loth to abandon it finally in the incomplete posture in which the fourth scene of this act left it. Ten lines in this scene sufficed to end the story, by relating the cure of the insane girl ; and there can have been no difficulty in their introduction, even on my supposition of this scene being the work of the other author. If the two wrote at the same time, the poet who wrote the rest of the scene may have inserted

(*Enter Palamon and his knights, pinioned; jailor, executioner, and guard.*)

Palamon. There's many a man alive that hath outlived
The love of the people; yea, in the self-same state
Stands many a father with his child; some com|fort
We have by so considering. We expire,—
And not without men's pity;—to live still,
Have their good wishes. We prevent
The loathsome misery of age, beguile
The gout and rheum, that in lag hours attend
For grey approachers. We come towards the gods
Young and unwarped, not halting under crimes
Many and stale; that sure shall please the gods
Sooner than such, to give us nectar with | them,—
For we are more clear spir|its! | .   .
  2 *Knight.*   Let us bid farewell;
And with our patience anger tottering for|tune,
Who at her certain'st reels.
  3 *Knight.*   Come, who begins?
  Palamon. Even he that led you to this banquet shall
Taste to you all.   .   .   .   .   .

  .   .   .   .
Adieu, and let my life be now as short
As my leave-taking.   (*Lies on the block.*)

If we were in a situation to give due effect to the supernatural part of the story, the miserable end of Palamon would affect us with a mingled sense of pity and indignation. He has been promised success by the divinity whom he adored, and yet he lies vanquished with the uplifted axe glittering above his head. Both the drama and Chaucer's poem assume the existence of such feelings on our part, and hasten to remove the cause of them. A way is devised for reconciling the contending oracles; and the catastrophe which effects that end, is, in the old poet, anxiously prepared by celestial agency.[1] Arcite has got the victory in the field, as his

---

them on the suggestion of the other; or if the drama afterwards came into the hands of that other, (which there seems some reason to believe,) he could easily insert them for himself. In any view these lines are no argument against my theory.

[1] The description which we have read of Mars's attributes reminds one strongly and directly of the fine speech in the poem, where old Saturn, the god of time, enumerates his own powers of destruction. It is far from unlikely that the one passage suggested the other. The rich can afford to borrow.

(side notes:)

Act V. scene vi. Weber; sc. iv. Littledale' Shakspere's.

(? Shakspere and one daughter.)

(Cf. p. 54-5.)

[page 55]

Chaucer' celestial agency to work out the plot.

Act V. scene vi.
(Weber ; sc. iv.
Littledale).

warlike divinity had promised him ; and an evil spirit is raised for
the purpose of bringing about his death, that the votary of the
Queen of Love may be allowed to enjoy the gentler meed which
his protectress had pledged herself to bestow. These supernal
intrigues are, in the play, no more than hinted at in the way of metaphor.

A cry is heard for delay of the execution ; Perithous rushes in,
ascends the scaffold, and, raising Palamon from the block, an-
nounces the approaching death of Arcite, with nearly the same
circumstances as in the poem. While he rode townwards from the
lists, on a black steed which had been the gift of Emily, he had
been thrown with violence, and now lies on the brink of dissolution.

[¹ page 56]
Description of
Arcite's mishap is
bad, but
Shakspere's.

The speech which describes Arcite's misadventure has been much
noticed by the critics, and by some lavishly praised. With de-
ference, I think it decidedly bad, but undeniably the work of
Shakspeare. The whole manner of it is that of some of his long

Over-laboured,
involv'd, hard,
yet Shakspere's,
with his words
and thoughts.

and over-laboured descriptions. It is full of illustration, infelicitous
but not weak ; in involvement of sentence and hardness of phrase
no passage in the play comes so close to him ; and there are traceable in one or two instances, not only his words, but the trains of
thought in which he indulges elsewhere, especially the description
of the horse, which closely resembles some spirited passages in the
Venus and Adonis. It is needless to quote any part of this speech.

End of the *Two
Noble Kinsmen.*

The after-part of this scene, which ends the play, contains some
forcible and lofty reflection, and the language is exceedingly vigorous and weighty. In Chaucer, the feelings of the dying Arcite are
expressed at much length, and very touchingly ; in the play, they
are dispatched shortly, and the attention continued on Palamon,
who had been its previous object :—

> (*Enter Theseus, Hippolita, Emilia, Arcite in a chair.*)
> *Palamon.*   Oh, miserable end of our alliance !
> The gods are mighty !—Arcite, if thy heart,
> Thy worthy, manly heart, be yet unbroken,
> Give me thy last words.   I am Palamon,
> One that yet loves thee dying.
> *Arcite.*   Take Emilia,
> And with her all the world's joy.   Reach thy hand :

Farewell ! I've told my last hour. I was false, Act V. scene vi.
But never treacherous : Forgive me, cous|in ! (Weber ; sc. iv.
Littledale).
One kiss from fair Emilia !—'Tis done :
Take her.—I die !
Palamon. Thy brave soul seek Elys|ium !

    .   .   .   .   .

   Theseus. His part is played ; and, though it were too short, Shakspere.
He did it well. Your day is lengthened, and
The blissful dew of heaven does arrose | you :
The powerful Venus well hath graced her al|tar,
And given you your love ; our master Mars
Hath vouched his oracle, and to Arcite gave
The grace of the contention : So the de|ities
Have shewed due justice.—Bear this hence.
   Palamon.   Oh, cous|in !
That we should things desire, which do cost | us
The loss of our desire! that nought could buy [page 57]
Dear love, but loss of dear love !
   Theseus.   .   .   .   Palamon !
Your kinsman hath confessed, the right o' the la'dy
Did lie in you : for you first saw her, and
Even then proclaimed your fancy. He restord | her
As your stolen jewel, and desired your spir|it
To send him hence forgiven ! The gods my jus|tice
Take from my hand, and they themselves become
The executioners. Lead your lady off :
And call your lovers from the stage of death,
Whom I adopt my friends.—A day or two
Let us look sadly, and give grace unto
The funeral of Arcite ; in whose end,
The visages of bridegrooms we'll put on,
And smile with Palamon ; for whom, an hour,
But one hour since, I was as dearly sor|ry,
As glad of Arcite ; and am now as glad,
As for him sorry.—Oh, you *heavenly charm|ers !* Shakspere.
What things you make of us ! For what we lack,
We laugh ; for what we have, are sorry still ;
Are children in some kind.—Let us be thank|ful
For that which is, and with you leave disputes
That are above our question.—Let us go off,
And bear us like the time !
                        (*Exeunt omnes.*)

You have now before you an outline of the subject of this highly
poetical drama, with specimens which may convey some notion of
the manner in which the plan is executed. But detached extracts

cannot furnish materials for a just decision as to the part which Shakspeare may have taken even in writing the scenes from which the quotations are given. If I addressed myself to one previously unacquainted with this drama, I should be compelled to request an attentive study of it from beginning to end. Such a perusal would convince the most sceptical mind that two authors were concerned in the work ; it would be perceived that certain scenes are distinguished by certain prominent characters, while others present different and dissimilar features. If we are to assume that Fletcher wrote parts of the play, we must admit that many parts of it were written by another person, and we have only to inquire who that other was. Without recurring to any external presumptions whatever, I think there is enough in most or all of the parts which are evidently not Fletcher's, to appropriate them to the great poet whose name, in this instance, tradition has associated with his. Even in the passages which have been here selected, you cannot but have traced Shakspeare's hand frequently and unequivocally. The introductory views which I slightly suggested to your recollection, may have furnished some rules of judgment, and cleared away some obstacles from the path ; and where I have failed in bringing out distinctly the real points of difference, your own acute judgment and delicate taste must have enabled you to draw instinctively those inferences which I have attempted to reach by systematic deduction.

In truth, a question of this sort is infinitely more easy of decision where Fletcher is the author against whose claims Shakspeare's are to be balanced, than it could be if the poet's supposed assistant were any other ancient English dramatist. If a drama were presented to us, where, as in some of Shakspeare's received works, he had taken up the ruder sketch of an older poet, and exerted his skill in altering and enlarging it, it would be very difficult indeed to discriminate between the original and his additions. He has often, especially in his earlier works, and in his histories more particularly, much of that exaggeration of ideas, and that strained and labouring force of expression, which marked the Hercules-like infancy of the English Drama. The stateliness with which Marlowe paces the

Marginal notes:

Two authors wrote *The Two Noble Kinsmen.*

Fletcher was one.

[¹ page 58]

The other was Shakspere.

Fletcher easily distinguisht from Shakspere.

Shakspere's Histories : their fault.

Marlowe.

tragic stage, and the magnificence of the train of solemn shews which attend him like the captives in a Roman procession of triumph, bear no distant likeness to the shape which Shakspeare's genius .assumes in its most lofty moods. And with those also who followed the latter, or trode side by side with him, he has many points of resemblance or identity. Jonson has his seriousness of views, his singleness of purpose, his weight of style, and his "fulness and frequency of sentence;" Massinger has his comprehension of thought, giving birth to an involved and parenthetical mode of construction; and Middleton, if he possesses few of his other qualities, has much of his precision and straightforward earnestness of expression.[1] In examining isolated passages with the view of ascertaining whether they were written by Shakspeare or by any of those other [2]poets, we should frequently have no ground of decision but the insecure and narrow one of comparative excellence. When Fletcher is Shakspeare's only competitor, we are very seldom driven to adopt so doubtful a footing; we are not compelled to reason from difference in *degree*, because we are sensible of a striking dissimilarity in *kind*. We observe ease and elegance of expression opposed to energy and quaintness; brevity is met by dilation, and the obscurity which results from hurry of conception has to be compared with the vagueness proceeding from indistinctness of ideas; lowness, narrowness, and poverty of thought, are contrasted with elevation, richness, and comprehension: on the one hand is an intellect barely active enough to seek the true elements of the poetical, and on the other a mind which, seeing those finer relations at a glance, darts off in the wantonness of its luxuriant strength to discover qualities with which poetry is but ill fitted to deal; in the one poet we behold that comparative feebleness of fancy which willingly stoops to the correction of taste, and in the other, that warmth, splendour, and quickness of imagination, which flows on like the burning rivers from a volcano, quenching all paler lights in its spreading radiance, and destroying every barrier which would impede or direct its devouring course. You will remark that certain passages or scenes in this play are attributed to Shakspeare, not because they are superior to Fletcher's

Marlowe's magnificence like Shakspere sometimes.

Jonson.

Massinger.

Middleton.

[2 page 59]

Fletcher and Shakspere contrasted.

They differ in *kind*.

Fletcher.

Shakspere.

Fletcher.

Shakspere.

Fletcher.

Shakspere.

Fletcher.

Shakspere.

---

[1] Beaumont's style is unluckily not characterized.—F.

tone or manner, but because they are unlike it. It may be true that most of these possess higher excellence than Fletcher could have easily reached; but this is merely an extrinsic circumstance, and it is not upon it that the judgment is founded. These passages are recognized as Shakspeare's, not from possessing in a higher degree those qualities in which Fletcher's merit lies, but from exhibiting other qualities in which he is partially or wholly wanting, and which even singly, and still more when combined, constitute a style and manner opposite to his.

Indeed, since Fletcher is acknowledged to stand immeasurably lower than Shakspeare, the excellence of some passages might perhaps in itself be no unfair reason for refusing to the inferior poet the credit of their execution. But an analysis of the means by which the excellence is produced places us beyond [1] the necessity of resorting, in the first instance at least, to this general ground or decision, which must, however, be taken into view, when we have been able to assume a position which entitles us to take advantage of it. In many parts of this play we find those external qualities which form Shakspeare's distinguishing characteristics, not separately and singly present, but combined most fully and most intimately; and it is consequently indisputable that we have, either Shakspeare's own writing, or a faithful and successful imitation of it. It is not easy to perceive with perfect clearness why it is that imitation of Shakspeare is peculiarly difficult; but every one is convinced that it is far more so than in the case of any other poet whatever. The range and opposition of his qualities, the rarity and loftiness of the most remarkable of these, and still more, the coincident operation of his most dissimilar powers, make it next to impossible, even in short and isolated passages, to produce an imitation which shall be mistaken for his original composition: but there is not even a possibility of success in an attempt to carry on such an imitation of him throughout many entire scenes. Where the external qualities of a work resemble his, the question of his authorship can be determined in no other way than by inquiring whether the essential elements, and the spirit which animates the whole, are his also; and that inquiry is not one for logical argument; it can be answered

Marginal notes:

Shakspere's work unlike Fletcher's.

Test between Shakspere and Fletcher.

[¹ page 60]

Shakspere's external qualities in the *Two Noble Kinsmen.*

Are they imitations?

Imitation of Shakspere difficult.

Why it is so.

Given, his outside dress,

ask whether his spirit is inside it.

only by reflection on the effect which the work produces on our own minds. The dullest eye can discriminate the free motions of the living frame from the convulsed writhings which art may excite in the senseless corpse; the nightly traveller easily distinguishes between the red and earthy twinkling of the distant cottage-lamp, and the cold white gleam of the star which rises beyond it ;—and with equal quickness and equal certainty the poetical sense can decide whether the living and ethereal principle of poetry is present, or only its corporeal clothing, its dead and inert resemblance. The emotion which poetry necessarily awakens in minds qualified as the subjects of its working, is the only evidence of its presence, and the measure and index of its strength. If we can read with coldness and indifference the drama which we are now examining, we must pronounce it to ¹be no more than a skilful imitation of Shakspeare ; but we must acknowledge it as an original if the heart burns and the fancy expands under its influence,—if we feel that the poetical and dramatic spirit breathes through all,—and if the mind bows down involuntarily before the powers of whose presence it is secretly but convincingly sensible. I cannot have a doubt that the parts of this work which I have pointed out as Shakspeare's will the more firmly endure this trial, the more closely and seriously they are revolved and studied.

The poetic sense alone can judge.

By the emotion it creates, must Shakspere's work be judgd.

[¹ page 61]

And his part of The Two Noble Kinsmen witnesses for itself.

The portions of the drama which, on such principles as these, have been set down as Shakspeare's, compose a large part of its bulk, and embrace most of the material circumstances of the story. They are,—the First Act wholly,—one scene out of six in the Third,—and the whole of the Fifth Act, (a very long one,) except one unimportant scene. These parts are not of equal excellence ; but the grounds on which a decision as to their authorship rests, seem to be almost equally strong with regard to each.

Shakspere's share of The Two Noble Kinsmen.

Act I.

Act III. sc. ⅰ.

Act V. except scene iv.

We have as yet been considering these scenes as so many separate pieces of poetry ; and they are valuable even in that light, not less from their intrinsic merit than as being the work of our greatest poet. If it be true merely that Shakspeare has here executed some portions of a plan which another had previously fixed on and sketched, the drama demands our zealous study, and is entitled to a place among

Shakspeare's works. An examination of separate details cannot enable us to form any more specific opinion as to the part which he may have taken in its composition.

Is the design of The Two Noble Kinsmen Shakspere's ?

But there is a further inquiry on which we are bound to enter, whatever its result may be,—whether it shall allow us to attribute to Shakspeare a wider influence over the work, or compel us to limit his claim to the subsidiary authorship, which only we have yet been able to establish for him. We must now endeavour to trace the design of the work to its origin ; we must look on the parts in their relation to the whole, and investigate the qualities and character of that whole which the parts compose. Such an analysis is essential to an appreciation of the real merit of the drama, and suggests

['page 62]

views of far-greater interest than any which offer themselves in the examination of isolated passages. And it is likewise necessary as a part of the inquiry which is our object, not merely because it may tend to strengthen or modify the decisions which we have already formed, but because it will allow us to determine other important questions which we have had no opportunity of treating. It will justify us, if I mistake not, in pronouncing with some confidence, that this drama owes to Shakspeare much more than the composition

Yes, it is.

of a few scenes,—that he was the poet who chose the story, and arranged the leading particulars of the method in which it is handled.

Before we enter the extensive and interesting field of inquiry thus opened to us, it may be well that I explain the reasons which

The tragic-comic underplot not Shakspere's.

seem distinctly to exclude from Shakspeare's part of the work one considerable portion of it,—the whole of the tragi-comic under-plot. I have as yet assigned no ground of rejection, but inferiority in the execution ; but there are other reasons, which, when combined with that, remove all uncertainty. Slightly as this subordinate story has been described, enough has been said to point out remarkable imitations of Shakspeare, both in incident and character. The insane maiden is a copy of Ophelia, with features from ' Lear ' ; the comments of the physician on her sickness of the mind, are borrowed

in conception from ' Macbeth '; the character of the fantastic schoolmaster is a repetition of the pedagogue in ' Love's Labour Lost'; and
the exhibition of the clowns which he directs, resemble scenes both
in that play and in the ' Midsummer Night's Dream.' All these circumstances together, or even one of them by itself, are enough to
destroy the notion of Shakspeare's authorship. The likeness which
is found elsewhere to Shakspeare's style, (and which is far closer in
those other parts of the play than it is here,) is an argument, as I
have shewn, in favour of his authorship ; the likeness here in
character and incident is even a stronger one against it. In neither
of these latter particulars does Shakspeare imitate himself as he
does in style. In some of his earlier plays indeed we may trace the
rude outlines of characters, chiefly comic, which he was afterwards
able to develope with [1] greater distinctness and more striking features ;
but though the likeness, in those cases, were nearer and more frequent than it is, the transition from the rude block to the finished
sculpture is the allowable and natural progress of genius. The bare
reproduction of a figure or a scene already drawn with clearness and
success, stands in a very different situation ; and, even if it should
be nearly equal to the original in actual merit, it creates a strong
presumption of its being no more than the artifice of an imitator.
Where the inferiority of the execution is palpable, the doubt is
raised into certainty. In the case before us, it is impossible to
receive the idea of Shakspeare sitting down in cold blood to imitate
the Ophelia, and to transfer all the tenderness of her situation to a
new drama of a far lower tone, in which also it should occupy only
a subordinate station. He could not have been guilty of this ; he
neither needed it, nor would have done it of free will ; and, therefore, I could not have believed it to be his, though the execution
had been far better than it is. But the inferiority is decided ; the
imitation produces neither vigour of style nor depth of feeling ; in
short, Shakspeare, if he had made the attempt, could not have
failed so utterly. The comic parts are only subservient to the
serious portion of this story ; and if Shakspeare did not write the
leading part, he was still less likely to have written the accessory ;
but, besides, the imitation is equally unsuccessful ; and the original

Fletcher's
borrowings in the
underplot, from
Shakspere.

Shakspere
doesn't imitate
himself in charac-
ter as he does in
style.

[1 page 63]

He doesn't re-
produce a figure
badly.

Shakspere could
not have turnd
his Ophelia into
the Jailer's
daughter of *The
Two Noble
Kinsmen.*

This Daughter is
an utter failure.

of the schoolmaster is said to have been a personal portrait, which was very unlikely to have been repeated by the first painter after the freshness of the jest was gone. I have been the more anxious to place in its true light the question as to this part of the drama, because, on its seeming likeness to Shakspeare, Steevens founds an ingenious hypothesis, by which he endeavours to account for the origin of the tradition as to Shakspeare's concern in the play. That this is a designed imitation of Shakspeare is abundantly clear ; and it is not difficult to see why it is an unsuccessful one. Fletcher possesses much humour, but it is of a cast very unlike Shakspeare's, and very unfit to harmonise with it, or to qualify him for the imitation which he has here attempted. Why he made the attempt, we shall be able to discover only when the freaks of caprice, and of poetical caprice, [1]the wildest of all, shall be fully analyzed and fully accounted for. All that I have to prove is, that this portion of the work is not, and could not have been, Shakspeare's.

I have said that I consider as his, both the selection of the plot, and much of its arrangement. As to the Choice of the Subject, my position is, that in this particular, Shakspeare stands in unequivocal opposition to Jonson, Beaumont and Fletcher, and those others, contemporary with him, or a little his juniors, with whom his name is generally associated. I can easily shew that this opposition to the newer school in the choice of stories exists in Shakspeare individually ; and this would be enough for my purpose ; but I will go a little farther than I am called on, because I conceive him to share that opposition with some other poets, and because views open to us from this circumstance, which are of some value for the right understanding of his characteristics. I say then, that in the choice of subjects particularly, as well as in other features, Shakspeare belongs to a school older than that of Fletcher, and radically different from it. The principle of the contrariety in the choice of subjects between the older and newer schools, is this : the older poets usually prefer stories with which their audience must have been previously familiar ; the newer poets avoid such known subjects, and attempt to create an adventitious interest for their pieces, by appeal-

The Schoolmaster is not Shakspere's.

Fletcher's designd imitation of Shakspere.

[1 page 64]
The underplot not Shakspere's.

Shakspere's choice of subjects for his Plays.
He differs from his chief contemporaries and successors.

He belongs to the old school.

Shakspere took old stories ;

new poets new ones.

ing to the passion of curiosity, and feeding it with novelty of incident. The early writers may have adopted their rule of choice from a dis- *Early Plays founded on* trust in their own skill: but they are more likely to have been influenced by reflecting on the inexperience of their audience in theatrical exhibitions. By insisting on this quality in their plots, they hampered themselves much in the choice of them; and the subjects which offered themselves to the older among them, were mainly confined to two classes, history and the chivalrous tales, *History and Tales of Chivalry.* being the only two cycles of story with which, about the time of Shakspeare's birth, any general familiarity could be presumed. That such were the favourite themes of the infant English drama is abundantly clear, even from the lists of old lost dramas which have been preserved to us. By the time when Shakspeare stepped into [1]the *[¹ page 65]* arena, the zeal for translation had increased the stock of popular knowledge by the addition of the classical fables and the foreign *Classical fables and foreign novels.* modern novels; and his immediate precursors, some of whom were men of much learning, had especially availed themselves of the former class of plots. If, passing over Shakspeare, we glance at the plots of Fletcher, Jonson, or others of the same period, we find, *Plots of Shakspere's successors.* among a great diversity of means, a search for novelty universally set on foot. Jonson is fond of inventing his plots; Beaumont and Fletcher usually borrow theirs; but neither by the former nor the latter were stories chosen which were familiar to the people, nor in any instance perhaps do they condescend to use plots which had been previously written on. Where Beaumont and Fletcher do *Beaumont Fletcher's.* avail themselves of common tales, they artfully combine them with others, and receive assistance from complexity of adventure in keeping their uniform purpose in view. The historical drama was re- *Historical Drama grew obsolete.* garded by the new school as a rude and obsolete form; and there are scarcely half a dozen instances in which any writer of that age, but Shakspeare, adopted it later than 1600. Historical subjects indeed wanted the coveted charm, as did also the Romantic and the Classical Tales, both of which shared in the neglect with which the Chronicles were treated. The Foreign Novels, and stories partly *Plots were got from foreign novels and invention.* borrowed from them, or wholly invented, were almost the sole subjects of the newer drama, which has always the air of addressing itself to hearers possessing greater dramatic experience and more extended information than those who were in the view of the older writers.

Shakspeare, in point of time, stood between these two classes : does he decidedly belong to either, or shew a leaning, and to which ? He unequivocally belongs to the older class ; or rather, the opposition to the newer writers assumes in him a far more decided shape than in any of his immediate forerunners ; for in them are found numerous exceptions to the rule, in him scarcely one. He returns, in fact, to more than one of the principles of the old school, which had begun in his time to fall into disuse. The external form of some of his plays, particularly his histories, is quite in the old taste.

The narrative chorus is the most observable remnant of antiquity ; and the long rhymed pas¹sages frequent in his earlier works, are abundant in the older writers : Peele uses them through whole scenes, and Marlowe likewise to excess. His continual introduction

of those conventional characters, his favourite jesters, is another point of resemblance to the ruder stage. And his choice of subjects, when combined with the peculiarities of economy just noticed, as

well as others, clearly appropriates him to the school of Lodge, Greene, and those elder writers who have left few works and fewer names. His Historical Plays are the perfection of the old school, the only valuable specimens of that class which it has produced, and the latest instance in which its example was followed ; and he has had recourse to the Classical story for such subjects as approached most nearly to the nature of his English Chronicles. And you must take especial note, that, even in the class of subjects in which he seems to coincide with the new school,—I mean his Plots borrowed from Foreign Novels,—he assumes no more of conformity than its

appearance, while the principle of contrariety is still retained. The new writers preferred untranslated novels, and, where they chose translated ones, disguised them till the features of the original were

lost : Shakspeare not only uses translated tales—(this indeed from necessity)—and closely adheres to their minutest circumstances, but in almost every instance he has made.choice of those among them which can be proved to have been most widely known and esteemed at the time. Most of his plots founded on fanciful subjects, whether derived from novels or other sources, can be shewn to have been previously familiar to the people. The story of 'Measure for Measure' had been previously told ; that of 'As you Like It', he might have had from either of two popular collections of tales ; the fable of 'Much Ado about Nothing' seems to have been widely spread, and those of 'All's Well that Ends Well', and 'The Winter's Tale' ; 'Romeo and Juliet' appears in at least one collection of English novels, and in a poem which enjoyed much popularity. These are sufficient as examples ; but a still more remarkable circumstance is this. In repeated instances, about twelve in all, Shakspeare has chosen subjects on which plays had been previously written ; nay more, on the subjects which he has so re-written, he has produced some of his best dramas, and one his very masterpiece. 'Julius Cæsar' belongs to this list ; '*Lear*' does so likewise ; and 'HAMLET.' Is not that a singular fact ? I can use it at present only as a most valuable proof that the view which I take is an accurate one. But Shakspeare has also, oftener than once, applied to the chivalrous class of subjects, which was exclusively peculiar to the older school. Its tales indeed bore a strong likeness to his own most esteemed subjects of study ; for, amidst all their extravagancies and inconsistencies, the Gothic romances and poems, the older of them at all events, professed in form to be chronicles of fact, and in principle to assume historical truth as their groundwork. 'Pericles' is founded on one of the most popular romances of the middle ages, which had been also versified by Gower, the second father of the English poetical school. The characters in 'The Midsummer Night's Dream' are classical, but the costume is strictly Gothic, and shews that it was through the medium of romance that he drew the knowledge of them ; and the 'Troilus and Cressida' presents another classical and chivalrous subject, which Chaucer had handled at great length, also invested with the richness of the romantic garb and decoration.

Fletcher and Shakspeare being thus opposed to each other in their choice of subjects, what qualities are there in the Plot of The Two Noble Kinsmen, which may appropriate the choice of it to either ? In the first place, it is a chivalrous subject,—a classical

Marginal notes:

6 Plays of Shakspere founded on well-known stories.

12 on subjects of former Plays.

[¹ page 67]

3 on Classical subjects turnd into romances.

Shakspere chose the story of the *Two Noble Kinsmen.*

Fletcher would neither have chosen Chaucer's classical story for his plot, — story which had already been told in the Gothic style. The nature of the story then could have been no recommendation of it to Fletcher. He has not a single other subject of the sort ; he has even written one play in ridicule of chivalrous observances ; and the sarcasm of that humorous piece[1], both in the general design and the particular references, is aimed solely at the prose romances of knight-errantry, a diseased and posthumous off-shoot from the parent-root, whose legitimate and ancient offspring, the metrical chronicles and

nor an old story,

[2 page 68]

tales, he seems neither to have known nor cared for. Secondly, this story must have been unacceptable to Fletcher, because it was a fa[2]miliar one in England. This fact is perhaps sufficiently proved by its being the subject of that animated and admirable poem of Chaucer, which Dryden has pronounced little inferior to the Iliad or Æneid ; but it is still more distinctly shewn by a third fact, which completely clenches the argument against Fletcher's choice

nor one on which two 16th-century plays had been written.

of it as a subject. No fewer than two plays had been written on this story before the end of the sixteenth century ; the earlier of the two, the Palamon and Arcite of Edwards, acted in 1566, and printed in 1585, and another play called by the same name, brought on the stage in 1594.[3]

Fletcher didn't choose the subject of *The Two Noble Kinsmen.*

It is thus, I think, proved almost to demonstration, that the person who chose this subject was not Fletcher ; and what has been already said, even without the specific evidence of individual passages, creates a strong probability that the choice was made by Shakspeare rather than by any other dramatic poet of his time. If the question be merely one between the two writers,—if, assuming it to be proved that Shakspeare wrote parts of the play, we have only to ask which of the two it was that chose the subject,—we can surely be at no loss to decide. But the presumption in Shakspeare's favour may be elevated almost into absolute certainty, while, at the same time, some important qualities of his will be illustrated,—if we

Shakspere's study of chivalrous poetry.

inquire what was the real extent to which he attached himself to the study of the chivalrous poetry, from which this subject is taken, and

---

[1] The Knight of the Burning Pestle.

[3] Weber's Beaumont and Fletcher. Henslowe MSS. published by Malone :
—Boswell's Shakspeare, vol. iii. p. 303. [See Appx. I. to my Harrison *Forewords.*]

the influence which that study was likely to have had, and did actually exercise on his writings.

If, being told that a dramatic poet was born in England in the latter half of the sixteenth century, whose studies, for all effectual benefit which they could have afforded him, were limited to his own tongue, we were asked to say what course his acquisitions were likely to have taken, our reply would be ready and unhesitating. English literature was of narrow extent before the time in question, and, according to the invariable progress of mental culture, had been evolved first in those finer branches which issue primarily from the imagination and affections, and appeal for their effect to the principles in which they have their source. Poetry had reached a vigorous youth, history was in its infancy, philosophy had not come into being. Had the field of study been wider, it was to poetry in an especial manner that a poet had to betake himself for an experience and skill in his art, and in the language which was to be its instrument. And it was almost solely to the narrative poets that Shakspeare had to appeal for aid and guidance; for preceding writers in the dramatic walk could teach him little. They could serve as beacons only, and not examples, and he had to search in other mines for the materials to rear his palace of thought. But the English poetical writers who preceded him are all more or less impressed with the seal of the Gothic school, and the most noted among them belong to it essentially. Chaucer, Lydgate, and Gower, to more than one of whom Shakspeare is materially indebted, were the heads of a sect whose subjects and form of composition were varied only as the various forms and subjects of the foreign romantic writers. The rhymed romance, the metrical vision, the sustained allegorical narrative or dialogue, were but differing results of the same principle, and forms too of its original development; for Britain was the mother and nurse of much of the finest chivalrous poetry, as well as the scene where some of its most fascinating tales are laid. It is true that English poetry before the time of Elizabeth presents but few distinguished names; but there is a world of unappropriated treasures of the chivalrous class of poetry, which are still the delight of those who possess the key to their secret cham-

Shakspere certain to have
[¹ page 69]
first studi'd, and been influenct by, our old narrative poets,
who were of the Gothic school.
Britain the mother of much fine chivalrous poetry.

bers, and were the archetypes of the earlier poets of that prolific age. It is important to recollect, that among the poets who adorn

Spenser belongs to the Gothic school.

that epoch, the narrative preceded the dramatic. Spenser belongs, in every view, to the romantic or Gothic school ; the heroic Mort d'Arthur was the rule of his poetical faith ; and it was that school, headed by him, which Shakspeare, on commencing his course and choosing his path, found in possession of all the popularity of the

Shakspere too.

day. Every thing proves that he allowed himself to be guided by the prevailing taste. His early poems belong in design to Spenser's

[¹ page 70]

school, and their style is ¹often imitative of his. In his dramas he has many points of resemblance to the older chivalrous poets, besides

[N.B. The Gower choruses in *Pericles* are NOT Shakspere's.—F.]

his occasional adoption of their subjects. His respect for Gower is shewn by the repeated introduction of his shade as the speaker in his choruses ; and particular allusions and images, borrowed from Gothic usages and chivalrous facts, occur at the first blush to the recollection of every one. But there is a more widely spread influence than all this. Many of his most faulty peculiarities are directly drawn from this source, and his innumerable misrepresentations or

Shakspere's mistakes and

mistakes are not so truly the fruit of his own ignorance, as the necessary qualities of the class of poets to which he belonged, shared with him by some of the greatest poetical names which modern

anomalies, those of his Gothic school.

Europe can cite. In this situation are indeed almost all the irregularities and anomalies which have furnished the unbelievers in the divinity of his genius with objects of contemptuous abuse ;—his creation of geographies wholly fictitious,—his anachronisms in facts and customs,—his misstatements of historical detail,—his dukes and kings in republics,—his harbours in the heart of continents, and his journies over land to remote islands,—his heathenism in Christian lands and times, and his bishops, and priests, and masses, *in partibus infidelium.* We may censure him for these irregularities if we

Chaucer and Spenser had the like.

will ; but it is incumbent on us to recollect that Chaucer and Spenser must bear the same sentence : and if the faults are considered so weighty as to shut out from our notice the works in which they are found, the early literature, not of our own country only, but of the whole of continental Europe, must be thrown aside as one mass of unworthy fable.

In truth, Shakspeare, in throwing himself on a style of thought and a track of study which exposed him to such errors, did no more than retire towards those principles which not only were the sources of poetry in his own country, but are the fountains from which, in every nation, her first draughts of inspiration are drunk.   Poetry in its earlier stages is universally neither more nor less than a falsifying of history.   The decoration of the Real is an exertion of the fancy which marks an age elder than the creation of the purely Ideal ; it is an effort more successful than the [1]attempt which follows it, and the wholly fictitious has always the appearance of being resorted to from necessity rather than choice.   Cathay is an older and fitter seat of romance than Utopia ; and the historical paladins and soldans are characters more poetical than the creatures of pure imagination who displaced them.   But this walk of poetry is one in which she never can permanently linger ; her citadel indeed is real existence partially comprehended, but she is unable to defend the fortress after knowledge has begun to sap its outworks ; she needs ignorance for her ally while she occupies the domain of history, and when that companion deserts her, she unwillingly retreats on the Possible and Invented, where she has no enemy to contest her possession of the ground.—While however she does continue in her older haunt, she must sometimes wander out of her imperfectly defined path, and her errors will depend, both in kind and in amount, on the amount and kind of her knowledge.   That the qualities of poetical literature, in every nation, are dependent on the number and species of those experiences from which in each particular case the art receives its materials, is indeed too evident to need illustration ; but some curious inferences are deducible from an application of this truth to the contrast which is found between the poetical literature of modern Europe, and that older school which has been called the classical. The inherent excellencies of the ancient Greek poetry may yet remain to be accounted for from other causes ; but this one principle was adequate to produce the most distinguishing qualities of the pagan literature, while it is distinctly the very same principle, acting in different circumstances, which has given birth to the opposite character of the modern school of invention.   During the period

Marginal notes:

Poetry is first a falsifying of History,

['page 71]

and has Ignorance as her ally.

(With Knowledge comes the retreat to Invention.)

Her errors depend on the kind of her small knowledge.

And hence come distinctive qualities of the Greek and Modern School.

Middle-Age

knowledge of
vast extent,

but never
thorough.

So it invested
History with in-
congruous attri-
butes.

[¹ page 72]

Early modern
poets invented a
national and
original
literature,

．

but, knowing
classics badly,

grafted on their
own works
excrescences
from classical
literature,

and on History,
fictions and mis-
takes.

which witnessed the gradual rise of that anomalous fabric of poetry, from whose prostrate fragments the perfected literature of Christian Europe has been erected, knowledge (I am uttering no paradox) was of vast extent; it embraced many different ages and many distant regions : but it was also universally imperfect; much was known in part, but nothing wholly.   Hence proceeded the specific difference of that widely-spread form of poetical invention, namely, the super-abundance and incongruity of attributes with which ¹it invested historical truth; and it is not very difficult to discover why many of those attributes have never thoroughly amalgamated with the princi-pal mass.   The various sources from which the materials of the romantic poetry were drawn, present themselves at once to every mind.   By the peculiar state of their knowledge, and the rude activity of spirit which was its consequence, the early poets of modern Europe were prepared to invent a species of literature which should be strictly national in its subjects, and in its essential parts wholly original.   That new branch was exposed, however, to modifi-cations of various kinds.   One temptation to introduce foreign elements, by which its authors were assailed, was singularly strong, and can scarcely in any other instance have operated on a literature arising in circumstances otherwise so favourable to originality, as those in which they were placed.   That temptation was offered by the imperfect acquaintance with the classical authors which formed one part of their scattered and ill-reconciled knowledge.   They were influenced by this cause, as they could not have failed to be ; and the representations of feelings, habits, and thought, which they borrowed from this source, being in their nature dissimilar to the constituent parts of the system to which they were adjected, never could have harmonised with these, and, under any circumstances, must have always continued to be excrescences.   Other elements of the new system were naturally neither evil in themselves, nor incon-sistent with the principles with which it was attempted to combine them, but have assumed the aspect of deformity and incongruity solely from incidental and extraneous causes.   The fictions and mis-takes which the ignorance of those fathers of our modern poetical learning superinduced on history ancient and modern, and on every thing which related to the then existing state either of the material world or of human society, were allowable ornaments, so long as knowledge afterwards acquired did not stamp on them the brand of falsehood; but the moment that the falsity was exposed, and the charm of possible existence broken, those adjuncts lost their empire over the imagination, and with it their appearance of fitness as materials for mental activity. In supernatural invention, the early *Supernaturalism of the Romantic* romantic poets [1] were still more unfortunate; for when they endea- *Poets* voured to colour with imaginary hues the awful outlines of the true *['page 73]* faith, they attempted a conjunction of holiness with impurity, an identification of the spirit with the flesh, a marriage between the living and the dead; the purer essence revolted from the union, and the human mind could acquiesce in imagining it only while it re- *only believable* *by superstition.* mained bound in the darkness and fetters of religious corruption. Turn now to the Grecian poetry, and mark how closely the same *Characteristics of* *early Greek* principles have operated on it, although the difference of the circum- *poetry.* stances has made the result different. The first Grecian inventors were, it is true, protected in a great measure from the influence of any foreign literature, simply by the ignorant rudeness of those ages of the world during which their task was performed; and even here I have no doubt that an influence not very dissimilar did actually operate; for there seems to be good reason for supposing that, if we had before us the wild songs of such bards as the Thracian Orpheus, or the old Musæus, we should find them strongly marked by that *Its tendency to* *orientalism;* orientalism towards which the later Greek poetry which remains to us betrays so continual a tendency. In other respects, the spirit in which the Greeks formed their poetical system was identical with our own. Their elder poets falsified historical facts, invented or disguised historical characters, and framed erroneous representations *its falsification of* *History,* of the past in time and the distant in place, no otherwise than did the romantic fabulists; and the classical inventors continued to have sufficient faith placed in their fictions, merely because knowledge advanced too slowly to allow detection of their falsity so long as the literature of the nation continued to exist for it as a present posses- sion. With their religious belief, again, every attractive invention *its treatment of* *Religion.* harmonised, and every splendid addition was readily incorporated as a consistent part ; where all was false, a falsity the more was unperceived or uncensured, and where sublimity and beauty were almost the only objects sought, they were gladly accepted from whatever quarter or in whatever shape they came.

So far as these considerations seem to elucidate the principles on which Shakspeare proceeded, they do so by exhibiting him as with-drawing from his own times as to his subjects and the ex¹ternal form of his works, though not as to their animating spirit,—as placing himself delightedly amidst the rude greatness of older poetry and past ages, and viewing life and nature from their covert, as if he had sat within a solitary and ruined aboriginal temple, and looked out upon the valley and the mountains from among those broken and massive columns, whose aspect gave majesty and solemnity to the landscape which was beheld through their moss-grown vistas. So far as these views have any force as a defence of faults detected in the great poet, that defence is founded on the consideration that the errors were unavoidable consequences of the system which produced so much that was admirable, and that they were shared with him by those whom he followed in his selection of subjects and form of writing. So far as all that has been said on this head has a close application to the main subject of our inquiry, its sum is briefly this. An argument arises in favour of Shakspeare's choice of the plot of this drama, from its general qualities, as a familiar and favourite story, and one of a class which had been frequently used by the older dramatists ; that argument receives additional strength from the fact of this individual subject having been previously treated in a dramatic form ; and it is rendered almost impregnable when we consider the subject particularly as a chivalrous story, and as belonging and leading us back to that native school to which Shakspeare, though in certain respects infected by the exotic taste of the age, yet in essentials belonged,—the wilderness in which Chaucer had opened up the well-head of poetry, where Gower and Lydgate had drunk freely, and Sackville had more sparingly dipped his brow,—the paradise through which Spenser had joyfully wan-dered with the heavenly Una,—the patriarchal forest into which afterwards Milton loved to retire from his lamp-lighted chamber, to

[¹ page 74]

Shakspere, for his stories and form, left his own time, and de-lighted in the past.

Thence his faults.

Summary of reasons why Shakspere chose the plot of *Two Noble Kinsmen*.

He went back to the school of

Chaucer

and Spenser ;

which Milton, after, sought.

sleep at the foot of some huge over-hanging oak, and dream of
mailed knights riding by his resting-place, or fairy choirs dancing on
the green hillocks around,—the enchanted rose-garden where Shakspeare himself gathered those garlands of beauty, which he has
described as adding glory even to his thoughts of love.

Shakspere's love
of old poems.

> [1] When in the chronicle of wasted time
> I see description of the fairest wights,
> *And beauty making beautiful old ryme*
> In praise of ladies dead and lovely knights;
> Then in the blazon of sweet beauty's best,
> Of hand, of foot, of lip, of eye, of brow,
> I see this antique pen would have expresst
> Even such a beauty as you master now.   *Sonnet* 106.

[1 page 75]

    In the Arrangement of the Plot also there are circumstances
which point emphatically to Shakspeare's agency.   One strong argument is furnished by a very prominent quality of the plot as it is
managed,—its simplicity.   This quality is like him, as being in this
case the result of a close adherence to the original story; but it is
also like him in itself, since the arrangement of all his works indicates the operation of a principle tending to produce it, namely, a
reliance for dramatic effect on the execution of the parts rather than
on the mechanical perfection or complication of the whole.   His
contemporaries, in their own several ways, bestowed extreme care
on their plots.   With Beaumont and Fletcher, hurry, surprise, and
rapid and romantic revolution of incident are the main object, rather
than tragic strength or even stage effect: their plays would furnish
materials for extended novels, and are often borrowed from such
without concentration or omission.   Shakspeare's comparative
poverty of plot is not approached by them even in their serious
plays, and the lively stir of their comic adventures is the farthest
from it imaginable.   Jonson's plots are constructed most elaborately
and admirably: one or two of them are without equal for skill of
conduct and pertinency and connection of parts.   This cautious and
industrious poet never confided in his own capability of making up
for feebleness of plan by the force of individual passages; and his
distrust was well judged, for the abstract coldness of his mind be-

Shakspere seen
in the simplicity
of the plot.

He relied on the
execution of the
parts, not the
complication of
the whole.

Beaumont and
Fletcher's plots
depend more on
surprise and
incident.

B. Jonson's plots
admirably con-
structed.

trays itself in every page of his dialogue, and his scenes need all their beauty of outline to conceal the frigidity of their filling up. Ford and Massinger agree much in their choice of plots, both preferring incidents of a powerfully tragic nature : but their modes of

Ford's gloomy plots softened by tenderness

[¹ page 76]

management are widely different. Ford, on the gloom of whose stories glimpses 'of pathos fall like moonlight, delights, when he comes to work up the details of his tragic plan, in softening it down into the most dissolving tenderness ; at his bidding tears flow in situations where we listen rather to hear Agony shriek, or look to behold Terror freezing into stone ; his emotion is not the rising vehemence

and regret.

of present passion, but the anguish, subsiding into regret, which lingers when suffering is past, and suggests ideas of eventual resignation and repose ;—his verse is like the voice of a child weeping

Massinger's stage effect by situations,

itself to sleep. Massinger crowds adventure upon adventure, and his situations are wound up to the height of unmixed horror ; for stage effect and tragic intensity, some of them, as for example the last scene in 'The Unnatural Combat', and the celebrated one in 'The Duke of Milan', are unequalled in the modern drama, and worthy of

and tragic design.
His coldness of expression.

the sternness of the antique ; but it is in the design alone that the tragic spirit works ; the colouring of the details is cold as monumental marble ; the pomp of lofty eloquence apes the simplicity of grief, or silence is left to interpret alike for sorrow or despair. To the carefulness in outlining the plan and devising situations, thus shewn in different ways, Shakspeare's manner is perfectly alien. He never exhausts himself in framing his plots, but reserves his strength

Shakspere's great aim to bring out character and feeling.

for the great aim which he had before him, the evolution of human character and passion, a result which he relied on his own power to produce from any plot however naked. He does not want variety of adventure in many of his plays ; but he has it only where his novel or chronicle gave it to him : he does not reject it when it is offered, but does not make the smallest exertion to search for it.

Shakspere's plays with no plot :

The Tempest.

Some of his plays, especially his comedies, have actually no plot, and those, too, the very dramas in which his genius has gained some of its most mighty victories. 'The Tempest' is an instance : what is there in it ? A ship's company are driven by wreck upon an island ; they find an old man there who had been injured by certain of them,

and a reconciliation takes place. The only action of 'As You Like *As You Like It.*
It' is pedestrian ; if the characters had been placed in the forest in
the first scene, the drama would have been then as ripe for its
catastrophe as it is in the last. 'The Midsummer Night's Dream' *Midsummer Night's Dream* has no plot.
relates a midnight stroll in a wood ; and the unreal na¹ture of the in-
cidents is playfully indicated in its name. It is from no stronger [¹ page 77]
materials than those three frail threads of narrative that our poet
has spun unrivalled tissues of novel thought and divine fancy. And,
as in his lighter works he is careless of variety of adventure, so in
his tragic plays he does not seek to heap horrors or griefs one upon In the plots of Shakspere's
another in devising the arrangement of his plots. In this latter class Tragedies, details and character are
of his works, the skill and force with which the interest is woven out the main things.
of the details of story and elements of character, make it difficult for
us to see how far it is that we are indebted to these for the power
which the scene exerts over us. But with a little reflection we are
able to discover, that there is scarcely one drama of his, in which,
from the same materials, situations could not have been formed, He could have made more strik-
which should have possessed in their mere outline a tenfold amount ing effect out of *Hamlet,*
of interest and tragic effect to those which Shakspeare has presented Acts IV. & V. 4.
to us. 'Hamlet' offers, especially in the two last acts, some remarkable proofs of his indifference to the means which he held in his
hands for increasing the tragic interest of his situations, and of the
boldness with which he threw himself on his own resources for the
creation of the most intense effect out of the slenderest outline.
But no example can shew more strikingly his independence of tragic
situation, and his power of concocting dramatic power out of the
most meagre elements of story, than the third act of the Othello. *Othello,* Act III.
It contains no more than the development and triumph of the
devilish design which was afterwards to issue in murder and remorse ;
and other writers would have treated it in no other style than as
necessary to prepare the way for the harrowing conclusion. In the
Moor's dialogues with Iago, the act of vengeance, ever and anon
sternly contemplated, and darkening all with its horror, is yet but
one ingredient in the misery of the tale. These scenes are a tragedy
in themselves, the story of the most hideous revolution in a noble
nature ; and their catastrophe of wretchedness is complete when

the tumult of doubt sinks into resolved and desolate conviction,—
when the Moor dashes Desdemona from him, and rushes out in
uncontrollable agony.—-Read also the conclusion of Lear, and learn
the same lesson from the economy of that most touching scene.
The horrors which have gathered so thickly 'throughout the last act,
are carefully removed to the background, and free room is left for
the sorrowful groupe on which every eye is turned.   The situation
is simple in the extreme ; but how tragically moving are the internal
convulsions for the representation of which the poet has worthily
husbanded his force !   Lear enters with frantic cries, bearing the
body of his dead daughter in his arms ; he alternates between
agitating doubts and wishing unbelief of her death, and piteously
experiments on the lifeless corpse ; he bends over her with the
dotage of an old man's affection, and calls to mind the soft lowness
of her voice, till he fancies he can hear its murmurs.   Then succeeds
the dreadful torpor of despairing insanity, during which he receives
the most cruel tidings with apathy, or replies to them with wild in-
coherence ; and the heart flows forth at the close with its last burst
of love, only to break in the vehemence of its emotion,— commencing
with the tenderness of regret, swelling into choking grief, and at
last, when the eye catches the tokens of mortality in the dead, snap-
ping the chords of life in a paroxysm of agonised horror.

> Oh, thou wilt come no more ;
> Never, never, never, never, never !
> —Pray you, undo this button : Thank you, Sir.—
> Do you see this ?—*Look on her—look*—HER LIPS !
> *Look there !   Look there !*

The application here of the differences thus pointed out is easy
enough.   Fletcher either would not have chosen so bare a story, or
he would have treated it in another guise.   The incidents which
constitute the story are neither many nor highly wrought : they are
only the capture of the two knights,—their becoming enamoured of
the lady,—the combat which was to decide their title to her,—and
the death of Arcite after it.   And no complexity of minor adventures
is inserted to disturb the simplicity so presented.   In all this there
is nothing which Fletcher could have found sufficient to maintain

Margin notes:

So in the end of *Lear,*

['page 78]

all is left clear for the one group, the father and his dead child.

Incidents of *The Two Noble Kinsmen* story

wouldn't have suited Fletcher.

that continuity and stretch of interest which he always thought necessary. He would have invented accessory circumstances, he would have produced new characters, or thrust the less important person¹ages who now fill the stage, further into the foreground, and more constantly into action : the one simple and inartificial story which we have, possessing none of his mercurial activity of motion, and scarcely exciting a feeling of curiosity, would have been transformed into a complication of intrigues, amidst which the figures who occupy the centre of the piece as it stands, would have been only individuals sharing their importance with others, and scarcely allowed room enough to make their features at all distinguishable. He'd have added to 'em. [¹ page 79]

In the management of particular scenes of this play, likewise, certain circumstances are observable, which, separately, seem to go a certain length in establishing Shakspeare's claim to the arrangement, and have considerable force when taken together. The second scene of the first act would appear to have been sketched by him rather than Fletcher, from its containing no activity of incident, and serving no obvious purpose but the development of the character and situation of the two princes ; a mode of preparation not at all practised by Fletcher. Neither does any consequence flow from the beautiful scene immediately following ; a circumstance which points out Shakspere as having arranged the scene, and would strengthen the evidence of his having written the dialogue, if that required any corroboration. The bareness and undiversified iteration of situation in the first three scenes of the last act form one presumption against the devising of those scenes by Fletcher. The economy of the fifth scene of that act, in which Emilia, left alone on the stage, listens to the noise of the combat, is also, to me, strongly indicative of Shakspeare. The contrivance is unusual, but extremely well imagined. I do not recollect an instance in Fletcher bearing the smallest likeness to it, or founded on any principles at all analogous to that which is here called into operation. In Shakspeare, I think we may, in more than one drama, discover something which might have given the germ of it. He has not only in his historical plays again and again regretted the insufficiency of the means possessed by his stage, or any other, for the representation of such Shakspere's handling seen in certain scenes of *The Two Noble Kinsmen.* Act I. scene ii. design'd by Shakspere. Act I. scene iii. also. And Act V. scenes i. ii. iii. [? Emilia with the pictures.] Act V. scene v. also design'd by Shakspere.

Shakspere's
expedients for
avoiding spec-
tacles; in

[¹ page 80]
1 *Henry IV.*,

spectacles; but in several of those plays he has devised expedients for avoiding them. In 'Henry V.' we have the battle of Azincour; but the only encounter of ¹the opposite parties is that of Pistol and the luckless Signor Dew. In 'the first part of Henry IV.' he has shewn an unwillingness to risk the effect even of a single combat; for in the last scene of that play, where prince Henry engages Hotspur, the spectator's attention is distracted from the fight between them, by the entrance of Douglas, and his attack on the prudent

Richard II.,

Falstaff. In 'Richard II.' the lists are exhibited for the duel of Bolingbroke and Norfolk, which is inartificially broken off at the very last instant by the mandate of the king. But a more deeply marked

Emilia in *Two
N. K.* I. v.,
like Lady Mac-
beth in II. ii. of
Macbeth.

likeness to the spirit in which the scene in 'The Two Noble Kinsmen' is arranged, meets us in Lady Macbeth watching and listening while her husband perpetrates the murder, like a bad angel which delays its flight only till it be assured that the whispered temptation has done its work. And in this combat scene, even the ancient and artless expedient used, of relating important events by messengers brought in for that sole end, and having no part in the action, may be noticed as belonging to an older form of the drama than Fletcher's, and as being very frequently practised by Shakspeare himself.

The motives of
the play of
The Two N. K.

In quitting our cursory examination of the qualities which distinguish the mechanical arrangement of the play, we may advert to the mode in which those influences are conceived which give motion to the incidents of the story, and regulate its progress. The

Dramatic art
defin'd.

dramatic art is a representation of human character in action; and action in human life is prompted by passion, which the other powers of the mind serve only to guide, to modify, or to quell. In the conception of the passions which are chiefly operative in this drama, there seems to be much that is characteristic of a greater poet than

In *The Two
N. K.* the moving
passions are Love
and Jealousy.

Fletcher. In the first place, the passions which primarily originate the action of the piece are simple; they are Love and Jealousy; the purest and most disinterested form of the one, and the noblest and

This conception
is Shakspere's.

most generous which could be chosen for the other. The conception is Shakspere's in its loftiness and magnanimity; and it is his also as being a direct appeal to common sympathies, modified but slightly by partial or fugitive views of nature. But it also resembles him in the singleness and coherence of design with [1]which the idea is seized and followed out. It cannot be necessary that I should specifically exemplify the closeness with which those ruling passions are brought to bear on the leading circumstances of the story from first to last. And it is almost equally superfluous to remind you, how far any such adherence to that unity of impulse, operates as evidence in a question between the two poets whom we have here to compare. Fletcher, in common with other poets of all ranks inferior to the highest, is unable to preserve any one form of passion or of character skilfully in the foreground : he may seem occasionally to have proposed to himself the prosecution of such an end, but he either degenerates into the exhibition of a few over-wrought dramatic contrasts, or loses his way altogether amidst the complicated adventures with which he incumbers his stories. This inability to keep sight of an uniform design, is in truth one striking argument of inferiority ; and the clearness with which Shakspeare conceives a definite purpose, and the fixedness with which he pursues it, go very far to unravel the great secret of his power. I have already pointed out to you, perhaps without necessity, wherein it is that his strength of passion consists ; that it is not in the incidents of his fable, but in his mode of treating the incidents ; that he will not rely on mere vigour or skill of outline in his stage-grouping, for that influence which he is conscious of being always able to acquire more worthily, by the beauty and emotion which he breathes into the organic formation of the living statuary of the scene ; that he refuses to sacrifice to the meretricious attraction of strained situations or entangled incidents, the internal and self-supporting strength of his historical pictures of the heart, or the unflinching accuracy of his demonstrations of the intellectual anatomy. In a similar way you will look for his unity of purpose, not in the mechanical economy of his plots, but in the elementary conception of his characters, and in his developement of the principles of passion under whose suggestions those characters act. He chooses as the subject of his delineation some mightily and truly conceived impersonation of human attributes, in-

The keeping close to the leading motives, is Shakspere's doing.
[' page 81]

Fletcher's inability to work a character out, to keep one passion always in the front.

Shakspere's definite purpose, and keeping to it.

His relying on the emotion he puts into his characters.

Shakspere's unity of purpose, seen in his conception, and his carrying this out.

Shakspere's
conception of
character, and
means and
method of de-
veloping it.

['page 8a]

consistent it may be in itself, but faithful to its prototype as being
inconsistent according to the rules which guide inconsistency in our
enigmati¹cal mental constitution ; for the exhibition of the character
so imagined he devises some chain of events by which its internal
springs of action may be brought into play ; and he traces the
motion and results of those spiritual impulses with an undeviating
steadiness of design, which turns aside neither to raise curiosity nor
to gratify a craving for any other mean excitement. Some singular
instances of Shakspeare's fine judgment in clinging to one great

Desdemona's
murder compard
with Annabella's
(by Ford).

design, are furnished by the 'Othello.' The death of Desdemona has
been compared with the murder of Annabella, a scene (evidently
drawn from it) in a drama of Ford's on a story which makes the flesh

Ford's above
Shakspere's in
pathos.

creep. Some have pronounced Ford's scene superior in pathos to
Shakspeare's : I think it is decidedly so. The tender mournfulness
of the language and few images is exquisite, and the sweet sad
monotonous melody of the versification is indescribably affecting.
Is it from weakness that Shakspeare has not given to the death of
his gentle lady an equally strong impress of pathos ? No. He was
not indeed susceptible of the feminine abandonment of Ford; but
he was equal to a manly tone of feeling, fitted to excite a truer

Why ? Because
of Shakspere's
self-restraint.

sympathy. He has refused to stretch the chords of feeling to the
utmost in favour of Desdemona ; and his refusal has a design and
meaning in it. There is anguish in the scene, and the most utter

The mind of
Othello is the
centre of
Shakspere's
play,

yielding to overpowering sorrow ; but it is the Moor who feels those
emotions, and it is the exhibition of his mind which is the leading
end of this scene, as of the rest of the drama. The suffering lady
is but an inferior actor in the scene ; her situation is brought out
with perfect skill and genuine tenderness, so far as it is consistent

and the pathos of
Desdemona's
death must be
kept down.

with the first object and illustrative of it ; but its expression is ar-
rested at the point where its further developement would have
marred the effect of the scene as a whole, and broken in on its pervading spirit. Ford had no such aim in view ; and the very scene
of his which is so beautiful in itself, loses almost all its force when
regarded as a part of the play in which it is inserted.

These principles of Shakspeare's could be traced as influencing
the drama of the 'Two Noble Kinsmen,' even if there were nothing

farther to shew their effect than what has been already [1]noticed.   [' page 83]
But their power is displayed still more admirably in a second quality
in the mode of conception, less open to notice, but breathing
actively through all.   There is skill in the mental machinery which
gives motion to the story; but there is even greater art in the application of a hidden influence, which controls the action of the
moving power, and equalizes its effects.   That secret principle is
Friendship, the operation of which is shewn most distinctly in the
Kinsmen, guiding every part of their behaviour except where their
mutual claim to Emilia's love comes into operation, never extinct
even there, though its effect be sometimes suspended, and awaken-
ing on the approach of Arcite's death, with a warmth which is
natural as well as touching.   But this feeling has a farther working:
Love of Friends is in truth the leading idea of the piece: the whole
drama is one sacrifice on the altar of one of the holiest influences
which affect the mind of man.   Palamon and Arcite are the first
who bow down before the shrine, but Theseus and Perithous follow,
and Emilia and her sister do homage likewise.   This singular harmony of parts was an idea perfectly beyond Fletcher's reach; and
the execution of it was equally unfit for his attempting.   The discrimination, the delicate relief, with which the different shades of
the affection are elaborated, is inimitable.   The love of the
Princesses does not issue in action; it is a placid feeling, which
gladly contemplates its own likeness in others, or turns back with
memory to the vanished hours of childhood: with Theseus and his
friend, the passion is exhibited dimly, as longing for exertion, but
not gifted with opportunity; and in the Kinsmen, it bursts out into
full activity, quelling all but the one omnipotent passion, and tem-
pering and purifying even it.   With this exception, you will not look
for much of Shakspeare's skill in delineating character.   The features of the two Princes are aptly enough distinguished; but neither
in them, nor in any of the others, is there an approach to his higher
efforts.   You will recollect that in his acknowledged works those finer
and deeper pryings into character have place only in few instances;
and that the greater number of his dramas depend for their effect
chiefly on other causes, some of which are energetic in this very play.

Shakspere's art in subduing all The Two Noble Kinsmen *to one Friendship.*

Love of Friends the leading idea of The Two Noble Kinsmen.

The harmony of its parts, an idea beyond Fletcher.

Not much of Shakspere's characterization in The Two Noble Kinsmen.

SPALDING.   6

['page 84]

[1]While you successively inspected particular passages in this play, your attention was necessarily called both to the character of its imaginative portions, and to the tone of reflection which is so frequently assumed in it. The drama having been now put entirely before you, I shall wish you to ponder its ruling temper as a whole,

Whose is the ruling temper of The Two Noble Kinsmen?

and to determine whether that temper is Fletcher's, or belongs to a more thoughtful, inquisitive, and solemn mind. When you institute such a reconsideration, I shall be desirous that you contemplate the internal spirit of the work from a loftier and more commanding station than that which you formerly occupied ; and I shall crave

Seek in it the mind of its author.

you to view its elements of thought and feeling less as the qualities of a literary work, than as the signs and results of the mental constitution of its author. I cannot regard as altogether foreign to our leading purpose any inquiry which may hold out the promise of illustrating the characteristics of Shakspeare even slightly, and of

The duty of our reverence for Shakspere, the Star of Poets, being intelligent.

teaching us to mingle a more active discernment in the reverence with which we look up to the Star of Poets from the common level of our unendowed humanity. You will therefore have the patience to accompany me in the suggestion of some queries as to the character of his mode of thinking, and the way in which his reflective spirit and his poetical qualities of mind are combined and influence each other. We may be able to perceive the more distinctly the real character both of his intellect and his poetical faculty, if you will consent that our investigation shall set out from a point which you may be inclined to consider somewhat more remote than is

We'll treat 1. the true functions of Poetry, 2. its true province.

altogether necessary. It is to be desired that we should have clearly in our view, first, the true functions of the poetical faculty, and, secondly, the province in poetical invention which legitimately belongs to the imagination, properly so called. Sound conclusions on both these points are indispensable to sound criticism on individual specimens of the poetical art ; and when we attempt to reason on particular cases, without having those conclusions placed prominently in view at the outset, the vagueness of ordinary language makes us constantly liable to lose sight of their true grounds and distinctions. The laying down of such principles at the institution of an inquiry

[² page 85]

into the poetical character of a great [2]poet, is therefore in no degree less useful, than the inculcating of familiar truths is in the instructions of religious and moral teachers ; the end in each of the cases being, not the establishing of new principles, but the placing of known and admitted ones in an aspect which shall render them influential ; and the necessity in each, arising from the danger which exists lest the principles, acknowledged in the abstract, should in practice be wholly disregarded.

We can in no way discover the real character and objects of the Poetical Art so easily as by contrasting it with the Arts of Design ; and the materials for such a comparison are afforded by the Laocoon of Lessing. The principles established in that admirable essay will scarcely be now disputed, and may be fairly enough summed up in the following manner.[1]—A study of the Grecian works of art convinces us, that "among the ancients Beauty was the presiding law of those arts which are occupied with Form ;" that, to that supreme object, the Greek artists sacrificed every collateral end which might be inconsistent with it ; and that, in particular, they expressed the external signs of mental commotion and bodily suffering, to no farther extent than that which allowed Beauty to be completely preserved. Now, that this subordination of Expression to Beauty is a fundamental principle of art, and not a mere accidental quality of Grecian art individually, is proved by considering the peculiar constitution and mechanical necessities of art. Its representations are confined to a single instant of time ; and that one circumstance imposes on it two limitations, which necessarily produce the characteristic quality of the Grecian works. First, " the expression must never be selected from what may be called the *acme* or transcendent point of the action ;" and that because, the power of the arts of design being confined to the arresting of a single point in the developement of an action, it is indispensable that they should select a point which is in the highest degree significant, and most fully excites the imagination ; a condition [2] which is fulfilled only by those points in an action in which the action moves onward, and the passion which prompts it increases ; and which is not fulfilled in any degree by the highest

Marginal notes:
Contrast of the Arts of Poetry and Design, in Lessing's *Laocoon.*

The Greeks subordinated Expression to Beauty.

And all Design must do the same, because

1. the expression must be caught before the highest passion is attaind :

[2 page 86]

---

[1] It would be unfair not to state, that I quote and refer to the translation of the Laocoon published by Mr. De Quincey, in Blackwood's Magazine for November 1826 ; and that I am not otherwise acquainted with that or any other work of Lessing.

2. because the expression must not be that of a momentary feeling.

stage of the passion and the completion of the action. Secondly, a limitation is imposed as to the choice of the proper point in the onward progress of the action : for art invests with a motionless and unchanging permanence the point of action which it selects ; and consequently any appearance which essentially possesses the character of suddenness and evanescence is unfit to be its subject, since the mind cannot readily conceive such transitory appearances as stiffened into that monumental stability.—Since it is by the limitation of the Fine Arts to the representation of a single instant of time that the two limitations in point of expression are imposed, and

But Poetry is not bound by the limits of the Fine Arts.

since Poetry is not subject to that mechanical limitation, but can describe successively every stage of an action, and every phasis of a passion, it follows that this latter art is not fettered by the limitation in expression, which is consequent on the physical limitation of the

It can seize passion at its height.

other ; and hence the exhibition of passion in its height is as allowable in poetry as it is inadmissible in the arts of design. And since the whole range and the whole strength of human thought, action, and passion, are thus left open to the poet as subjects of his repre-

Beauty is but one of its many resources.

sentation, it follows likewise, that Beauty " can never be more than one amongst many resources, (and those the slightest,) by which he has it in his power to engage our interest for his characters."

It will be remarked, that the purport of Lessing's reasoning, so far as he has in express terms carried it, is no more than to demonstrate the important truth, that the Fine Arts are confined by certain limits to which Poetry is not subject. His elucidation of the principles of poetry is purely incidental and negative. His reasoning seems however necessarily to infer certain further consequences, the examination of which has a tendency to cast additional light on the true end and character of the poetical art : and it is for this reason rather than from any difficulty lying in the way of those implied results, that I wish now to direct your notice to their nature, and the

[1 page 87]

grounds on which [1] their soundness rests. Lessing's second canon

Design must represent Form of permanent feelings.

does not assume the arts of design as pursuing any further end than their original and obvious one, the Representation of Form : it simply directs that only those appearances of form shall be represented which admit of being conceived as permanent. And as the feelings which art desires to awaken are pleasurable, and as forms, considered merely *as* forms, give pleasure only when they are beautiful, art would thus be regarded as proposing for its object nothing beyond a Representation of the Beautiful, and Verisimilitude in that representation. The first rule of limitation however implies a great deal more : it looks to forms, not as such, but as tokens significant of certain qualities not inherent in their own nature : for the quality which it requires to be possessed by works of art, is a capability of exciting the imagination to frame for itself representations of human action and passion ; and in this view, those feelings which the qualities of form considered as such are calculated to arouse, are no more than an accidental part of the impression which the representation makes. It appears, therefore, that art *may* pursue two different ends,—the excitement of the feeling which Beauty inspires, and the excitement of the feeling which has its root in human Sympathy ; and the question at once occurs,—Is each of these purposes of art equally a part of its original and proper province ? Or, since it is sufficiently clear that the effects which the last-mentioned canon contemplates as produced by the fine arts, are effects which are also produced by poetry, (whether its sole effects or not, it is immaterial to this question to settle,) the question may be put in another form : —Is it to be believed, that the arts of design, which have admittedly for one purpose the reproduction of the Beautiful in form, have also as an equally proper and original purpose the framing of representations of form calculated to affect the mind with feelings different from the feeling of the Beautiful,—these feelings being identically the same with those which are at least the most obvious effects of poetry ? Reasons crowd in upon the mind, evincing that the question must be answered by an unqualified negative. The production of poetical effects cannot have been an *original* purpose of the fine arts, which certainly were brought into existence [1] by the love of Beauty ; and the production of those effects is plainly also an exertion in which the fine arts overstep their limits, and wander into the region which belongs of right to the poetical art, and to it alone. That Expression in painting and sculpture is an extraneous and borrowed quality, is made almost undeniably evident by this

The object of Art, a true representation of the Beautiful.

May it also try to excite feelings inconsistent with the Beautiful,

as Poetry does ?

No.

[[1] page 88]

Expression in Painting and Sculpture is a borrowed quality

one consideration, that it requires, as we have seen, to be always kept subdued, and allowed to enter only partially into the composition of the work.   And, again, it is no argument against that position, to say that the strongest and most general interest and admiration are excited by those works of art in which expression is permitted to go the utmost length which the physical limits of the art permit.   For the universality of this preference only proves, that the feelings of our common humanity influence more minds than does the pure love of the beautiful; and the greater strength of the feeling produced by expression, only evinces that poetry, which works its effect by means of that quality, is a more powerful engine than the sister-art for stirring up the depths of our nature.   And it may be quite true that those works of art which confine themselves to the attempt to move the calmer feeling due to Beauty, are the truest to their own nature and proper aim, although an endeavour to unite with that the attainment of higher purposes may be admissible, and in some instances highly successful.   I apprehend that although an art should propose as its main end the production of one particular effect, it does not follow that its effects should be confined to the production of that alone, if its physical conditions permit the partial pursuit of others.   More especially, if an art should admit of uniting, to a certain extent, with its own peculiar and legitimate end, the prosecution of another loftier than the first, surely we might expect to find such an art occasionally taking advantage of the license; and yet its doing so would not compel us to say, that both these are its proper and original purposes.   And the fact is, that the attempt is seldom made; for very few works of classical art exist in which the union of the two principles is tried, the end sought being usually the representation of beauty, and that alone.   In no way, however, can the radical difference and opposition between the two qualities be evinced so satisfactorily as by a comparison [1] of the effects which they severally produce on the mind.   Expression, the poetical element, gives rise to a peculiar activity of the soul, a certain species of reflective emotion, which, it is true, is easily distinguishable from underived passion, and does not necessarily produce like it a tendency to action, but which yet essentially partakes of the character

That Fine Art is admired most when it has most expression, only shows that

Poetry stirs men more than pure Art does.

Fine Art *may* borrow from its loftier sister, Poetry,

but Classic Art very rarely does, and rightly.

[¹ page 89]

Expression belongs to Poetry. It excites.

of mental commotion, and is opposed to the idea of mental in- *Poetry stirs men.*
activity. The feeling which Beauty awakens is of a character entirely
opposite. The contemplation of the Beautiful begets an inclination *Beauty soothes them.*
to repose, a stillness and luxurious absorption of every mental fac-
ulty : thought is dormant, and even sensation is scarcely followed by
the perception which is its usual consequence. It is with this soft-
ness and relaxation of mind that we are inspired when we look on *Look at the Venus de Medici.*
such works as the Venus de Medici, in which beauty is sole and
supreme, and expression is permitted to be no farther present than
as it is necessary as an indication of the internal influence of soul,
that so those sympathies may be awakened, without whose partial
action even beauty itself possesses no power. If we turn to those
few works of ancient art, in which the opposite element is admitted, *When ancient art stirs you, as in the*
we are conscious that the soul is differently acted upon, and we may
be able by reflection to disentangle the ravelled threads of feeling,
and distinguish the mental changes which flow upon and through
each other like the successive waves on the sea-beach. In contem-
plating the Apollo, for instance, a feeling akin to the poetical, or *Apollo and*
rather identical with it, is awakened by the divine majesty of the
statue ; and upon the quiet and self-brooding luxury with which the
heart is filled by the perfect beauty of the youthful outlines, there
steals a more fervent emotion which makes us proud to look on the
proud figure, which makes us stand more erect while we gaze, and
imitate involuntarily that godlike attitude and expression of calm
and beautiful disdain. Or look to the wonderful Laocoon, in which *Laocoon,*
the abstract feeling of beauty is even more deeply merged in the *it is by their having left their own ground, and taken that of Poetry, Expression.*
human feeling of the pathetic,—that extraordinary groupe, in which
continued meditation arouses more and more actively the emotion
of sympathy, while we view the dark and swimming shadows of the
eyes, the absorbed and motionless agony of the mouth, and the tense
torture of the iron muscles of [1] the body. It is impossible to conceive *[¹ page 90]*
that an art can propose to itself, as originally and properly its own,
two ends so difficult of reconcilement and so different in the quali-
ties by which they are brought about. Finally, the Plastic Arts *Lastly, Fine Art appeals to sight.*
offer form directly to the sense of sight, whereas it is very doubtful
whether poetry can convey, even indirectly, any visual image. *Poetry never does.*

Consequently, the result of admitting Expression as a primary and legitimate end of the arts of form, would be to ascribe to them an innate and underived capability of presenting directly to the senses both beauty and the wide circle of human action and feeling; while the genius of Poetry, by her nature shut out from direct representation of the beautiful, whose shadows she can evoke only through the agency of associated ideas, would have even her own kingdom of thought and passion, her power as the great interpreter of mind, shared with her by a rival, whom the decision would acknowledge indeed as possessing a right to the divided empire, but who is disqualified by the nature of her instruments from exercising that sovereignty to the full.   And, on the other hand, by the acknowledgment that the arts of form are not properly a representation of human action or human passion, and that when they aim at becoming so, they attempt a task which is above and beyond their sphere, and in which their success can never be more than partial, Poetry is exhibited in an august and noble aspect, as stooping to lend a share in her broad and lofty dominion to another art of narrower scope, which is so enabled to gain over the mind an influence of transcending its own unassisted capacities.

If you shall be able to think this excursive disquisition justifiable, it will be because it insensibly leads us to perceive what truly is the legitimate and sole end of the Poetical Art, and because it thus clears the way for one or two elementary propositions regarding the functions of the Poetical Faculty.   First, we perceive that poetry does not aim at the representation of visual beauty.   I do not say that beauty may not form the subject of poetry: my meaning is, that the poet can depict it poetically in no way except by indicating its effects on the mind.   When poetry mistakingly attempts to represent beauty by its external form, its failure to affect the mind is signal and complete, and must be [1]so, even supposing it to be possible that the picture should be so full and accurate that the painter might sketch from it.   The reason of this is perhaps discoverable.   Such a description cannot affect the mind with the poetical sentiment, because it does not represent to the imagination those qualities by which it is that the poetical effect is

Marginal notes:
If Fine Art rightly includes Expression, then it has Beauty too;

while Poetry, which can't express Beauty directly, has to give up part of its province, Expression, to Art, which can't use it fully.

Poetry rather lends its help to its narrower ally, Art.

The aims of Poetry:

1. not to represent Beauty to the eye,

but only to the mind.

[1 page 91]

produced; and if it were to move the mind at all, it must be with those feelings which beauty excites when it is seen corporeally present. It fails to operate even this effect, and why? Beauty of form affects the mind through the intervention of sense; and the perception of the sensible qualities of form is followed instantaneously and necessarily by the pleasurable emotion. This mental process is involuntary, and the nature of the sentiment excited implies inactivity and absorption of the mind. When however the imagination is called on to combine into a connected whole the scattered features which words successively present, an effort of the will is necessary: and the failure in the pleasurable effect appears to be adequately accounted for (independently of any imperfection in the result of the combination) by the inconsistency of this degree of mental activity with the inert frame of mind which is requisite for the actual contemplation and enjoyment of the beautiful. When, again, the poet represents beauty in the method chalked out for him by the nature of his art, it is quite impossible that he can convey any distinct visual image; for he represents the poetical qualities by indicating them as the causes which produce some particular temper or frame of mind: and as every mind has its distinctive differences of association, a truly poetical picture is not realised by any two minds with precisely similar features. And the mood of mind to which this representation gives birth, is radically opposite to the other; it is active, sympathetic, and even reflective: we seem, as it were, to share the feeling with others, to derive an added delight from witnessing the manner in which they are affected, or even to have the original passive sentiment of pleasure entirely swallowed up in that energetic emotion.[1] Secondly,

Marginal notes: Contrast of the effects of Beauty and Expression, of Fine Art and Poetry, on the mind. — Beauty gives pleasure, rest, absorption. — Poetry stirs the Imagination, the Will, — disturbs the passiveness that Beauty produces. — It can't produce an image by sight, — but only by association. — Its effect is opposite to that of Beauty of Form.

[1] The theory which, denying to the Beautiful any capacity of giving pleasure through its innate qualities, ascribes its effects exclusively to the associated ideas which the contemplation of it calls up, proceeds wholly on the assumption, that the sentiment awakened by Beauty when it is beheld bodily present, is the same with that which flows from a poetical description of it. If it be true (as I must believe it is) that the feelings in the two cases are essentially different, the hypothesis falls to the ground. Its maintainers seem in truth to have drawn their conclusions altogether from reflection on the effects produced by Beauty when it is represented in poetry, where association is undoubtedly the source of the enjoyment; and an attention to the working of the fine arts would have taught other inferences.

[¹ page 92]

2. Poetry's true subject is Mind, and not external nature,

except as tinged with thought and feeling.

3. Poetry is analytical; it perceives, discriminates.

Its combinations depend on its first analysis.

4. Poetry depends on the power and accuracy of its perception of the poetical qualities in its materials.

[¹ page 93]

Of Imagination or Imagery.

the true subject of poetry is ¹ Mind. Its most strictly original purpose is that of imaging mind *directly*, by the representation of humanity as acting, thinking, or suffering; it presents images of external nature only because the weakness of the mind compels it; and it is careful to represent sensible images solely as they are acted on by mind. When it makes the description of external nature its professed end, it in truth does not represent the sensible objects themselves, but only exhibits certain modes of thought and feeling, and characterises the sensible forms no farther than as the causes which produce them. Thirdly, The most characteristic function of the poetical faculty is *analytical;* it is essentially a *perception*, a power of discovery, analysis, and discrimination. An object having been presented to it by the imagination, it discovers, and separates from the mass of its qualities, those of them which are calculated to affect the mind with that emotion which is the instrumental end of poetry. Coincidently with the perception and discovery of the qualities, it perceives and experiences the peculiar effect which each particular quality produces; and, lastly, it sets forth and represents those resulting moods of mind, indicating at the same time what those qualities of the object are through which they are excited. Its task of combination is no more than consequent on this process, and supposes each step of it to have been previously gone through. Fourthly, It follows, (and this is the result which makes the inquiry important,) that the poetical faculty is measured by the strength and accuracy with which it perceives the poetical qualities of those objects which the imagination suggests as its materials, and not by the number of the ideas so presented. A forgetfulness of this truth has occasioned more misapprehension and ² false criticism than any other error whatever ; and we are continually in danger of the mistake, from the extension of meaning which use has attached to the word imagination, that term being commonly employed to designate the poetical faculty. This extended application is perhaps unavoidable ; but it is on that account the more necessary to guard against the misconception always likely to arise from the original signification of the word, which we can never discard entirely from the mind in using it in a secondary sense.—You do not need to be reminded how completely the history of the poetical art evinces, that these positions, whether expressly acquiesced in or not, have been invariably acted on in the judgments which the world has pronounced in particular cases.   The inadequacy of a representation of forms by their external attributes to constitute poetical pictures, could be instanced from every bad poem which has ever been written ; and the great truth, that the external world is exhibited poetically only by being represented as the exciting cause of mental changes, has been illustrated in no age so singularly as in our own.   The writings of Wordsworth in particular have stretched the principle to the utmost extent which it can possibly sustain ; demanding a belief that all external objects are poetical, because all can interest the human mind : establishing the reasonableness of the assumption by the boldest confidence in the strength and delicacy with which the poetical perception can trace the qualities which awaken that interest, and the progress of the feeling itself ; and applying the poetical faculty to the transforming of every object of sense into an energetic, and as it were sentient, existence.   And attention is especially due to the decision which has always recognized, as the rule of poetical excellence, the operation of some power independent of mere wealth of imagination, ranking this latter quality as one of the lowest merits of poetry.   We are apt to forget that those minds whose conceptions have been the most strongly and truly poetical, are by no means those whose poetical ideas have been the most abundant ; that an overflow of poetical images has been coincident with an intense perception of their most efficient poetical relations only in a few rare instances ; and that it is precisely where the highest elements of the poetical are most active that [1] the imagination is usually found to offer the fewest images as the materials on which the poetical faculty should work.   It is enough to name Dante, or, a still more singular instance, Alfieri.   In both cases the poetical influence rests on the intensity of the one simple aspect of grandeur or passion in which a character is presented, and in both that simplicity is unrelieved and undecorated by any fulness of imagery.[2]

Describing forms by their outsides, is not Poetry.

They must be shown as exciting changes of Mind.

Wordsworth declares that all outward objects can do this,

and become sentient existences.

Mere wealth of imagery is of little worth.

The greatest poets use the fewest images,

[¹ page 94.

witness Dante,

Alfieri.

Their intensity is their secret.

[2] Alfieri appears to have himself perceived accurately wherein it is that his power lies, when he says, with his usual self-reliance : "Se la parola 'invenzione'

Application of
these principles
to the Drama.

The Passions are
the chief subjects
of Poetry.

They work more
alone in the
Drama than else-
where.

In Epic and
other poetry
relying only on
words, the effort
to turn them into
a picture hinders
their prompt
action.
['page 95]

Didactic poetry
is not true poetry,
but sermons in
verse.

Invention is
making a *new*
thing out of a
thing already
made.

These fundamental principles of the poetical art possess a closer application to Dramatic Poetry than to any other species. All poetry being directly or indirectly a representation of human character ; and human character admitting of appreciation only by an exhibition of its results in action ; and action being prompted by the passionate impulses of the mind, which its reflective faculties only modify or stay ; it follows that the Passions are the leading subjects of Poetry, which consequently must be examined in the first instance with a view to its strength and accuracy as a representation of the working and results of that department of the mind. The nature of the dramatic art allows this rule to be applied to it with the greatest strictness. The drama is the species which presents the essential qualities of poetry less mingled with foreign adjuncts than they are in any other species ; and there seems to be a cause, (independent of its mechanical necessities,) enabling it to dispense with those decorations which abound in other kinds of poetry. The acted drama presents its picture of life directly to the senses, and permits the imagination, without any previous exertion, to proceed at once to its proper task of forming its own combinations from the sensible forms thus offered to it ; and even when the drama is read, the office of the imagination in representing to itself the action and the characters of the piece, is an easy one, and performed without the necessity of great activity of mind. On the other hand, in the epic, or any other species of poetry which represents action by ¹words, and not by an imitation of the action itself, the imagination has at first to form, from the successively presented features of the poetical description, a picture which shall be the exciting cause of the poetical impression : this supposes considerable energy of thought, and the necessity of relief from that exertion seems to have suggested the introduction of images of external nature and the like, on which the fancy may rest and disport itself. Those classes of poetry which are either partially or wholly didactic, cannot receive a strict appli-

in tragedia si restringe al trattare soltanto soggetti non prima trattati, nessuno autore ha inventato meno di me." " Se poi la parola 'invenzione' si estende fino al *far cosa nuova di cosa già fatta*, io son costretto a credere che nessuno autore abba inventato piu di me."

cation of the principles of the pure art ; because they are not properly poetry, but attempts to make poetical forms serve purposes which are not poetical.

Our journey has at length conducted us to Shakspeare, of many of whose peculiar qualities we have been gaining scattered glimpses in our progress. We remark him adopting that species of poetry which, necessarily confined by its forms, is yet the noblest offspring of the poetical faculty, and the truest to the purposes of the poetical art, because it is the most faithful and impressive image of the mind and state of man. We find him seated like an eastern sovereign amidst those who have adopted this highest form of poetry ; and we cannot be contented that, in reverentially acknowledging his worthiness to fill the throne, we should render him only a hasty and undiscerning homage. A discrimination of the particular qualities by which his sway is mainly supported, is rendered the more necessary by that extraordinary union of qualities, which has made him what he is, the unapproached and the unapproachable.—We are accustomed to lavish commendations on his vast Imagination. Before we can perceive what rank this quality of his deserves to hold in an estimate of his character, we must understand precisely what the quality is which we mean to praise. If the term used denotes merely the abundance of his illustrative conceptions, it expresses what is a singular quality, especially as co-existent with so many other endowments, but useful only as furnishing materials for the use of the poetical power. If the word is meant to call attention to the strength and delicacy with which his mind grasps and embodies the poetical relations of those overflowing conceptions, (still considered simply as illustrative or decorative,) [1] the quality indicated is a rare and valuable gift, and is especially to be noted in an attempt to trace a likeness to his manner. Still however it is but a secondary ground of desert ; it is even imperfectly suited for developement in dramatic dialogue, and it frequently tempts him to quit the genuine spirit and temper of his scene. If, again, in speaking of the great poet's imagination, we have regard to the poetical character of many of his leading conceptions, to the ideal grandeur or terror of some of his preternatural characters, or even to the romantic loveliness which he

---

Shakspere again.

He takes to Drama, because it's the noblest and truest form of Poetry, the likest the mind of man.

And there he sits enthrond.

But why?

What does his Imagination mean?

his wealth of imagery?

of fancy, of conception?

[¹ page 96]

No.

Does Shakspere's imagination mean the grandeur or loveliness he has given some of his characters?

has thrown, like the golden curtains of the morning, over the youth and love of woman,—we point out a quality which is admirable in itself, and almost divine in its union with others so opposite, a quality to which we are glad to turn for repose from the more severe portions of his works,—but still an excellence which is not the most marked feature of his character, and which he could want without losing the essential portion of his identity. We could conceive, (although the idea is sacrilege to the genius and the altar of poetry,) we could conceive that 'The Tempest' had remained unwritten, that Miranda had not made inexperience beautiful by the spell of innocence and youth, that the hideous slave Caliban had never scowled and cursed, nor Ariel alighted on the world like a shooting-star,—we could dismiss alike from our memories the moon-light forest in which the Fairy Court revel, and the lurid and spectre-peopled ghastliness of the cave of Hecate,—we could in fancy remove from the gallery of the poet's art the picture which exhibits the two self-destroyed lovers lying side by side in the tomb of the Capulets,—and we could discard from our minds, and hold as never having been invented by the poet, all which we find in his works possessing a character similar to these scenes and figures ;—and yet we should leave behind that which would support Shakspeare as having pursued the highest ends of his art, and as having attained those ends more fully than any other who ever followed them : Richard would still be his ; Macbeth would think and tremble, and Lear weep and be mad ; and Hamlet would still pore over the riddle of life, and find in death the solution of its mystery. If it is to such characters as these last that we refer when we speak of the poet's power of imagination, and if we wish to designate by the word the force with which he throws himself into the conception of those characters, then we apprehend truly what the sphere is in which his greatness lies, although we either describe the whole of a most complicated mental process by naming a single step of it, or load the name of that one mental act with a weight of meaning which it is unfit to bear.

It is here, in his mode of dealing with human character, that Shakspeare's supremacy confessedly lies ; and the conclusions which

No.

We could give up

Miranda,

Ariel,

Juliet, Romeo,

and yet leave the true, the highest Shakspere behind, in Richard, Macbeth, Lear, Hamlet.

These show his Imagination, the force with which he throws himself into their characters.
[' page 97]

Shakspere's supremacy lies in his characterization.

we have reached as to the great purpose of poetry, allow us easily
to perceive how excellence in this department justifies the universal
decision, which places at the summit of poetical art the poet who is
pre-eminently distinguished by it.   What is there in Shakspeare's
view of human character which entitles him to this high praise? His
truth of painting is usually specified as the source of his strength ;
in what sense is he true to nature? Is that faithfulness to nature
consistent with any exercise of the imagination in the representation
of character? And how? And again, how does his reflective temper of mind harmonize with or arise out of the view of human life
which he takes?

Poetry, as we have seen, and dramatic poetry more strictly than
any other species, must be judged primarily as a representation of passion and feeling ; and when it is defective as such, it has failed in its
proper end.   Its prosecution of that end, however, is subject to two
important limitations. First, if it is to be in any sense a *true* representation of human action, it must represent human nature not partially,
but entirely ; it must exhibit not only the moving influences which
produce action, but also the counteracting forces which in real life
always control it.   It must be a mirror of the intellectual part of the
human mind, as well as of the passionate.   Secondly, if, possessing
the first requisite, truth, it is to be also an *impressive* representation,
(that is, such a representation as shall effect the ends of poetical art,)
it must set up an ideal and elevated standard to regulate its choice
of the class of intellectual endowment which is to form the foundation of the characters which it portrays.   We discover the cause of
Jonson's inferiority in his failure in obedience to the latter of these
rules, though he scrupulously complied with [1] the first : we discover
the prevailing defect of all the other dramatic writers of that period,
to consist in their neglect even of the first and subsidiary rule, which
involved a complete disregard to the other.—These latter have, as
well as Shakspeare, been proposed as models, from their close imitation of nature.   The merit of truth to nature belongs to them only
in a very confined sense.   They seize one oblique and partial aspect
of human character, and represent it as giving a true and direct view
of the whole ; they are the poets of the passions, and no more ; they

Why is his the best?

How is he true to Nature and imagination?

Poetry (or Drama) represent passions.

But 1. it must show human nature entirely, both its moving and hindering forces ; man's mind as well as his passions ; 2. it must do this impressively, must have a high standard of character.

Ben Jonson faild in 2[1], the other Elizabethans in 1[1]. [1 page 98]

Shakspere's contemporaries don't imitate Nature, they distort it, give Passion, and no Reason.

have failed to shadow forth that control which the calmer principles of our nature always exert over the active propensities. Their excellence consequently is to be looked for only in scenes which properly admit the force of unchecked passion, or of passions conflicting with each other ; and in those scenes where the more thoughtful spirit ought to work, we must be prepared to meet either exaggeration of feeling or feebleness of thought, either the operation of an evil principle, or, at best, a defect of the good one. Even in their passionate scenes, the vigour of the drawing is the merit oftener than the faithfulness of the portrait ; they delight to figure the human mind as in a state of delirium, with the restraining forces taken off, and the passions and the imagination boiling, as if the brain were maddened by opiates or fever. Fierce and exciting visions come across the soul in such a paroxysm ; and in the intensity of its stimulated perceptions, it gazes down into the abysses of nature, with a profound though transitory quickness of penetration. It is a high merit to have exhibited those partial views of nature, or even this exaggerated phasis of the mind ; and the praise is shared by no dramatic school whatever ; (for the qualities of the ancient are different :) but it must not be assumed that the drama fulfils its highest purposes, by representations so partial, so distorted, or so disproportioned. As these poets of impulse bestowed no part of their attention on the intellect in any view, they produced their peculiar effect, such as it was, without any attempt at that higher task of selection and elevation in intellectual character for which the universality of views which they wanted must always serve as the foundation. They had accordingly little scope for the due introduction of reflection in their works ; and their turn of mind inclined them little to [1]search for it when it did not naturally present itself.—Jonson resembled Shakspeare in wideness of aim : he is most unlike him in the method which he adopted in the pursuit of his end. The two stood alone in their age and class, as alone aiming at truth to nature in any sense ; both wished to read each of the opposite sides of the scroll of human character : but the one read correctly the difficult writing in which intellectual character is traced, while the other misapprehended and misinterpreted its meaning, and even allowed the

They like to show the mind in delirium.

They are poets of impulse.

['page 99] Ben Jonson as broad in aim as Shakspere.

Ben Jonson tried at truth to nature,

eagerness with which he perused this perplexing page, to withdraw his attention from the more easy meaning of the other. The fault of his characters as intellectual beings, is that they are individuals and no more ; faithful or grotesque portraits of reality, they are not touched with that purple light which affords insight into universal relations and hidden causes. His failure is shewn by its effect : his characters are not so conceived as to lead the mind to the comprehension of anything beyond their own individual peculiarities, or to elevate it into that region of active and conceptive contemplation into which it is raised by the finest class of poetry : he exhibited reality as reality, and not in its relation to possibility ; he even diverges into the investigation of causes, instead of seeing them at a glance, and indicating them by effects; he anatomised human life, and hung up its dry bones along the walls of his study. *but drew individuals only, portraits of reality, but no types,*

not poetic creations.

In the close obedience which Shakspeare rendered to each of these two canons, borne in upon his mind by the instantaneous suggestions of his happy genius, we may discover the origin of his tremendous power. To commence at the point where his adherence to the first and subsidiary rule is most slightly manifested, it is to be noticed, that his works are marked throughout by a predominance of the qualities of the understanding over the fancy and the passions. This is not true of the fundamental conception of the work, nor of the relations by which his characters are united into the dramatic groupes ; in these particulars the poetical faculty is allowed to work freely : but it is after the initial steps have been taken under her guidance, that the rule is committed to the sterner power of intellect. The stir of fancy often breaks through the restraints which hold it in check ; the warmth of feeling effervesces very unfrequently. The poet's personages ¹are all more or less marked by an air of quiet sense, which is extremely unusual in poetry, and incompatible with the unnecessary or frequent display of feeling ; and accordingly, his less important scenes, whether they be gay or serious, occupied in the business of the drama, or devoted to an exchange of witty sallies, possess, where they aim at nothing higher, at least a degree of intellectual shrewdness, which very often savours of worldly coldness. Viewed merely as increasing the effect of his passionate scenes, this prevail- *Shakspere's power lay in*

subordinating Fancy and Passion to Intellect.

[¹ page 100]

All his characters have quiet good sense.

Shakspere's shrewdness in his minor scenes.

His soberness gives force to his passion.

ing sobriety of tone gives him an incalculable advantage : passion in his works bursts out when it is let loose, like the spring of a mastiff

Shakspere's sober rationality.

unchained.   It is of this quality, his sober rationality, that we are apt to think when we acknowledge his truth of representation : and the excellence is indispensable to truth in any sense, because the want of it gives birth to imperfection and distortion of views : but I apprehend that it is to his aiming at a higher purpose that we have to look for the genuine source of his power.   While we mark the gradual rise of the intellectual element of poetical character upwards

But he didn't reproduce the bare reality.

from its lowest stage, we are in truth approximating to a rule which issues in something beyond a bare and unselected reproduction of

Poetry aims at

reality.   Poetry aims at representing the whole of man's nature ; and yet a picture of human character, embracing all its features, but neither skilfully selecting its aspect nor majestically combining its

general truth,

component parts, would not effect the ends of poetry : for that art contemplates not individual but general truth, not that which is really produced, but that which may be conceived without doing violence

brings out the relation of one mind to universal nature ;

to acknowledged principles ; instead of presenting a bare portraiture of mental changes, it exhibits them in an aspect which teaches their relation to the system of universal nature ; it is seemingly conversant with facts, but it imperceptibly hints at causes ; it aims at exciting the imagination to frame pictures for itself, and for that reason, if

it idealizes and ennobles realities.

for no other, it must be permitted to idealize and ennoble the individual realities from which its materials are collected.   The mode in which poetry affects the mind is illustrated by the description

A Painting pictured a soldier in the midst of foes, yet showd him alone. [¹ page 101]

which we read of a certain ancient painting.   That piece represented a young soldier surrounded by several enemies and desperately defending himself ; but his own figure alone was ¹admitted into the field of view, and the motions and place of his unseen enemies were indicated solely by the life, energy, and significance of the attitude in which he was drawn.   Shakspeare's attachment to truth of representation never tempted him to forget the true purpose of his art.

Shakspere is true to nature in Poetry's way.

While he is true to nature by attempting the treatment of his whole subject, he is true to it in the manner and with the restrictions which the nature of poetry requires ; he is true to principles which admit of being conceived as producing effects, not to effects individually observed as resulting; the creatures of his conception possess no qualities which unfit them for exciting the mind as poetical charac- *His characters* ter should excite it; they are not repulsive by the unexampled and unatoned-for congregation of evil qualities, not mean by the absence *are not monsters* of lofty thought, not devoid of poetical significance by confining the *of evil,* imagination to the qualities by which they are individually marked. You will particularly remark, that, while he had to bring out the features of his characters by subjecting them to tragic and calamitous *nor are they* events, he was careful not to figure them as unsusceptible of the *above the influ-* influence of those external evils. The lofty view which he took of human nature did indeed admit the idea of a resistance to calamity, and a triumph over it, based on internal and conscious grandeur; but this is an aspect in which he does not present the human mind; the stoical Brutus is the only character in which he has attempted *Brutus is his one* such a conception, which he has there developed but partially. But *stoical character.* while he was contented, even in his noblest characters, to represent passion in all its strength and directed towards its usual objects, he had open to him sources of tragic strength unknown to those poets who describe passion only. Where passion alone is represented, no spectacle is so agitating as the conflict of contending passions; and the narrowness of such views of nature permits that tragic opposition to be no further exhibited. Shakspeare had before him a wider *Shakspere dealt* field of contrast—the conflict between the passions and the reason *not with the con-* *flict of Passions* —a struggle between powers inspired with deadly animosity, and *only, but with* *the strife between* each, as he conceived them, possessed of gigantic strength. He has *the Passions and* worthily represented that terrible encounter, engaging every principle *the Reason,* and faculty of the soul, and shaking the whole kingdom of man's *convulsing the* being with ¹internal convulsions. It is in such representations that *whole being of* *man.* his power is mainly felt; and his pictures are at the same time *[¹ page 102]* *In this is his* truest to nature and most faithful to the ends of tragic art, by *greatest power* *shown—as in* the subjugation of the intellectual principle which is the catas- *Othello and* trophe of the strife. The reason is assaulted by calamity from *Lear.* without, and borne down by an host of rebellious feelings attacking it internally. It is to the delineation of such characters as afford *Characters show-* *ing this mental* scope for this exhibition of mental commotion that Shakspeare *strife, are* *specially dear to* has especially attached himself: the thoughtful and reflective in *Shakspere.*

character is at once his favourite resort, and the field of his triumph.

He chose the intellectual and reflective in character.
The poet's selection of the intellectual and reflective in character, as the subject of his art, is thus indicated as his guiding principle, to whose operation all other principles and rules are but subservient. The reflective element however is in excess with Shakspeare, and its undue prevalence is not destitute of harmony with the principle which produces its legitimately moderated effects.

He's a Gnomic Poet.
He is a Gnomic Poet; and he is so, because he is emphatically the poet of man. He pauses, he reflects, he aphorizes; because, looking on life and death as he looked on them, viewing the nature of man from so lofty a station, and with a power of vision so far-reaching, so acute, and so delicate, it was impossible but the deep-

The solemnity of meditation is thro' all his soul.
est solemnity of meditation should diffuse itself through all the chambers of his soul. His enunciations of general truth are often serious and elevated even in his gayer works; and where the scene denied him an opportunity of introducing these in strict accordance

He makes his people hint the principles beneath the shews.
with the business of the drama, he makes his personages, as it were, step out of the groupe, to meditate on the meanings of the scene, to hold a delicately implied communication with the spectator, and to hint the general maxims and principles which lurk beneath the tragic and passionate shews. He has gone beyond this: he has brought on the stage characters whose sole task is meditation, whose sole purpose in the drama is the suggesting of high and serious reflec-

Jaques, in As You Like It, is like a Greek chorus, which
tion. Jaques is the perfection of such a character; and the office which he discharges bears more than a fanciful likeness in conception to the task of the ancient chorus. That forgotten appendage of the Grecian drama originated indeed from incidental causes; but,

being continued as a part of the dramatic plan, [1]it had a momentous duty assigned to it: it suggested, it interpreted, it sympathised, it

gave the key-note to the audience.
gave the key-note to the reflections of the audience. A profound sense of the highest purposes and responsibilities of the art prompted this employment of the choral songs; and no way dissimilar was

The highest art made Shakspere insert his reflective passages in his plays.
the impression which dictated to Shakspeare the introduction of the philosophically cynical lover of nature in that one play, and the breaks of reflection so frequent with him in many others.—It is

worthy of remark, that this spirit of penetrating thought, ranging from every-day wisdom to philosophical abstraction, never becomes morose or discontented.[1]   Man is a selfish being, but not a malignant one ; yet the acts resulting from the two dispositions are often very similar, and it is the error of the misanthrope to mistake the one for the other.   Shakspeare's well-balanced mind was in no danger of this mistake ; his keen-sightedness often makes him sarcastic, but the sarcasm forced on a mind which contrasts the poorness of reality with the splendours of imagination, is of a different temper from that which is bred from lowness of thought and fretful envy.   Shakspeare has devoted one admirable drama to the exhibition of the misanthrophic spirit, as produced by wrongs in a noble heart ; but the sternness which is the master-note of that work is softened by the most beautiful intervals of redeeming tenderness and good feeling.   The only work of his evidently written in ill humour with mankind, is the Troilus, which, both in idea and execution, is the most bitter of satires.

(r? in Jaques.)

Shakspere never made the misanthrope's mistake.

His sarcasm did not spring from envy.

Timon's

sternness is softend by tenderness.

Troilus is Shakspere's only bitter play.

The application of the distinctive qualities of Shakspeare's tone of thought to the spirit of ' The Two Noble Kinsmen', is a task for your own judgment and discrimination, and would not be aided by suggestions of mine.   I have stated the result to which I have been led by such an application ; and I am confident that you will be able to reach the same conclusion by a path which may be shorter than any which I could clear for you.   In connection however with this inquiry, I would direct your attention to one other truth possessing a clear application here.   Shakspeare's thoughtfulness goes the length of becoming a Moral distinction and excellence. That such a difference does exist between Shakspeare and Fletcher, is denied by no one ; and the moral tone of this play, in those parts which I have ¹ventured to call Shakspeare's, is distinctly a higher one than Fletcher's.   It is uniform and pure, though the moral inquisition is less severe than Shakspeare's often is.   If Massinger or Jonson had been the poet alleged to have written part or the whole of the work, it would have been difficult to draw any inference from this circumstance by itself ; but when the question is only between Shakspeare and Fletcher, even an abstinence

Shakspere's thoughtfulness a Moral distinction.

His part of *The Two Noble Kinsmen* is of higher tone, and purer, than Fletcher's.
[¹ page 104]

Massinger and Ben Jonson too more moral than Fletcher.

from gross violation or utter concealment of moral truth is an important element in the decision ; and the positively high strain here maintained is a very strong argument in favour of the purer writer.

Are Johnson, &c. right in condemning Shakspere's morality.

I am tempted, however, to carry you somewhat further on this head, because I must confess that I cannot see the grounds on which Johnson and others have rested their sweeping condemnation of Shakspeare's morality.   There is, it must be admitted, much to blame, but there is also something worthy of praise ; and praise on this score is what Shakspeare has scarcely ever received.

He admits licentiousness

He has been charged with licentiousness, and justly ; but even in this particular there are some circumstances of palliation, besides the equivocal plea of universal example, and the doubt which exists whether most of his grosser dialogues are not interpolations.   Mere

and coarse speech. But who can be tainted by Othello's words ?

coarseness of language may offend the taste, and yet be so used as to give no foundation for any heavier charge.   There surely never was a mind which could receive one evil suggestion from the language wrung from the agonized Othello.   Even where this excuse does not hold, Shakspeare preserves one most important distinction

Shakspere's contemporaries make their heroes loose livers.

quite unknown to his contemporaries.   By them, looseness of dialogue is introduced indifferently anywhere in the play, licentiousness of incident is admitted in any part of the plot, and debauchery of life is attributed without scruple to those persons in whom interest is chiefly meant to be excited.   It may be safely stated that Shak-

He doesn't,

speare almost invariably follows a rule exactly opposite.   His inferior characters may be sometimes gross and sensual ; his principal personages scarcely ever are so : these he refuses to degrade needlessly, by attributing to them that carelessness of moral restraint of which Fletcher's men of pleasure are so usually guilty.   There

except in two plays. [² page 105]

are only two plays[1] in which he [2]has violated this rule, exclusively of some unguarded expressions elsewhere.

But the language which has been held on this question would lead us to believe that his guilt extends further,—that he is totally insensible to any moral distinctions, and blind to moral aims and

---

[1] ? *All's Well*, Bertram ; *Othello*, Cassio ; *Meas. for Meas.* Claudio ; *Ant. & Cleop.* Antony ; *Timon*, Alcibiades.—F.

influences. Of most dramatic writers of his time this charge is too true. Their characters act because they will, not because they ought, —for happiness, and not from duty :—the lowness of their aim may be disguised, but it is inherent, and cannot be eradicated. We might read every work of Fletcher's without discovering (if we were ignorant of the fact before) that there exists for man any principle of action loftier in its origin than his earthly nature, or more extended in its object than the life which that nature enjoys. But nothing of this is true as to Shakspeare. That his morality is of the loftiest sort cannot be asserted. He does not, like Milton, look out on life at intervals from the windows of his sequestered hermitage, only to turn away from the sight and indulge in the most fervent aspirations after immortal purity, and the deepest adoration of uncreated power; nor does he grovel in the dust with that ascetic humiliation and religious sense of guilt which overcame the strong spirit of Michel Angelo. But he shares much of the solemnity of moral feeling which possesses all great minds, though in him its influence was restrained by external causes. He moves in the hurried pageant of the world, and sometimes wants leisure to moralize the spectacle ; and even when he does pause to meditate, the world often hangs about his heart, and he thinks of life as men in action are apt to think of it. But moral truth, seldom lost sight of, is never misrepresented : evil is always described as being evil : the great moral rule, though often stated as inoperative, is always acknowledged as binding. Read carefully any of his more lofty tragedies, and ponder the general truths there so lavishly scattered ; and you will find that an immense proportion of those apophthegms have a moral bearing, often a most solemn and impressive one. Even in his lighter plays there is much of the same spirit : in all he is often thoughtful, and he is never long thoughtful without becoming morally didactic. This is much in any poet, and especially in a dramatist, who exhibits humanity directly as active, and is under continual temptations to forget what action tempts men to forget in real life. His neglect of duly distributing punishment and reward is no moral fault, so long as moral truth is kept sight of in characterizing actions, while that neglect is borrowed closely from reality. And the same thing is true

Side notes:

Most of Shakspere's contemporaries made pleasure the law of their heroes' lives.

Shakspere's morality not of the loftiest, not like Milton's and

Michel Angelo's.

He was in the world, and often of it,

but evil, to him, was evil, moral law was always shown supreme. Note the general moral truth in his Tragedies.

Even in Comedy his reflections are moral.

[¹ page 106]

Shakspere right in letting evil prevail, so long as he shows it evil.

of his craving wish for describing human guilt, and darkening even his fairest characters with the shadows of weakness and sin. The poetry which depicts man in action is then unfortunately truest when it represents him as most deeply enslaved by the evil powers which surround him. Different poets have proceeded to different lengths in the degree of influence which they have assigned to the evil principle: most have feared to draw wholly aside the veil which imagination always struggles to keep before the nakedness of man's breast; and Shakspeare, by tearing away the curtain with a harsher hand, has but enabled himself to add a tremendously impressive element of truth to the likeness which his portrait otherwise bears to the original. His view of our state and nature is often painful; but it is its reality that makes it so; and he would have wanted one of his strongest holds on our hearts if he had probed them less profoundly; it is by his unflinching scrutiny of mortal infirmity that he has forged the very strongest chain which binds us to his footstool. He reverences human nature where it deserves respect: he knows man's divinity of mind, and harbours and expresses the loftiest of those hopes which haunt the heart like recollections: he represents worthily and well the struggle between good and evil, but he feared to represent the better principle as victorious: he had looked on life till observation became prophetical, and he could not fable that as existing which he sorrowfully saw could never be. The milk of human kindness in the bosom of Macbeth is turned to venom by the breath of an embodied fiend; the tempered nobility and gentleness of the Moor are made the craters through which his evil passions blaze out like central fires; and in the wonderful Hamlet, hate to the guilty pollutes the abhorrence of the crime,—irresolution waits on consciousness,—and the misery of doubt clings to the solemnity of meditation. This is an awful representation of the human soul; but is it [1]not a true one? The sibylline volume of man's history is open before us, and every page of it is written in blood or tears. And not only are such views of human fate the truest, but they are those which are most fitted to arouse the mind to serious, to lofty, even to religious contemplation,—to guide it to the fountains of moral truth,—to lead it to meditations on the dark

Marginal notes:
Dramatic poetry is truest when it shows man most the slave of evil.
Shakspere bared man's soul,
and probed it to its depth.
This is why we hold to him.
He durst not paint good triumphant over evil, because he knew in life it was not so.
Macbeth,
Othello,
Hamlet, sink under their temptations.
And so do we. [1 page 7] Man's history is written in blood and tears.
Shakspere's view of life the fittest to give us to the truth.

foundations of our being,—to direct its gaze forward on that great journey of the soul, in which mortal life is but a single step.

Oftener than once in this inquiry, I have acted towards you like one who, undertaking to guide a traveller through a beautiful valley, should frequently lead him out of the beaten road to climb precipitous eminences, promising that the delay in the accomplishment of the journey should be compensated by the pleasure of extensive prospects over the surrounding region. Conduct like this would be excusable in a guide, if the person escorted had leisure for the divergence, and it would be incumbent on him if the acquisition of a knowledge of the country were one of the purposes of the journey; but in either case the labour of the ascents would be recompensed to the traveller, only if the landscapes presented were interesting and distinctly seen. For similar reasons, my endeavour to propose wider views than the subject necessarily suggested, has, I conceive, been fully justifiable; but it is for you to decide whether the attempt has been so far successful as to repay your exertions in attending my excursive steps. The first of our lengthened digressions has allowed us to combine the known facts as to the kind and amount of Shakspeare's studies, and to draw from them certain conclusions, which I cannot think altogether valueless, as to some distinctions between him and his dramatic coevals, and as to the source of some peculiarities of his which have been visited with heavy censure. In the second instance in which we have branched off from the main argument, we have been led to reflect on the most characteristic qualities of the poet's mode of thought. If there be any truth or distinctness in the hints which have been imperfectly and hastily thrown out on this head, your own mind will classify, modify, or extend them; and, never forgetting what is [1]the fundamental principle of the great poet's strength, you will regard that essential quality with the more lively admiration, when you discriminate the operations of the power from the working of those other principles which minister to it, and when you remark the number, the variety, the opposition of the mental faculties, which are all thus enlisted under the banners of the one intense and

Analogy of this inquiry.

Aims of this treatise:

1. from Shakspeare's studies, to distinguish between him and his coevals.

2. to trace the most characteristic qualities of his thought.

[¹ page 108]

Shakspere's variety of faculty.

He, the stern
inquisitor into
man's heart,

the anxious
searcher into
truth, is yet the
happiest creator
of beauty : the
' maker' of Ric.
III. and Iago as
well as Juliet
and Titania ; of
Macbeth as well
as Hamlet.

His faculties
early expanded
consistently,
and workt thro'
all his life
actively.
Homer ebbd,

Milton sank
poetry in
polemics.

[¹ page 109]

Shakspere alone
flowd full tide
on.

almost philosophical Perception of Dramatic Truth. That stern
inquisition into the human heart, which the finest sense of dramatic
perfection elevates into the ideal, and the richest fancy touches with
poetical repose, will awaken in your mind a softened solemnity of
feeling, like that under whose sway we have both wandered in the
mountainous forests which skirt our native river ; the continuous
and gloomy canopy of the gigantic pines hanging over-head like a
dungeon roof, while the green sward which was the pavement of the
woodland temple, and the lines of natural columns which bounded
its retiring avenues, were flooded with the glad illumination of the
descending sunset. We reflect with wonder that the most anxious
of all poetical inquirers into truth, is also the most powerful painter
of unearthly horrors, and the most felicitous creator of romantic or
imaginary beauty ; that the poet of Richard and Iago is also the
poet of Juliet, of Ariel, and of Titania ; that the fearfully real self-
torture, the judicially inflicted remorse, of Macbeth, is set in contrast
with the wildest figures which superstitious imagination ever conceived ; that on the same canvas on which Hamlet stands as a
personification of the Reason of man shaken by the assaults of evil
within him and without, the gates of the grave are visibly opened,
and the dead ascend to utter strange secrets in the ear of night.
But even this union is less extraordinary than the regular and un-
paralleled consistency with which the poet's faculties early expanded
themselves, and the full activity with which through life all continued
to work. Even the dramatic soul of Homer ebbed like the sea,
sinking in old age into the substitution of wild and minutely told
adventure for the historical portraiture of mental grandeur and
passionate strength. The youth of Milton brooded over the love
and loveliness of external nature ; it was not till his maturity of
years that he soared into the empyrean or descended sheer into the
secrets of the abyss ; and ¹advancing age brought weakness with it,
and quenched in the morass of polemical disputation the torch
which had flamed with sacred light. Shakspeare alone was the
same from youth to age ; in youth no imperfection, in age no mortality or decay ; he performed in his early years every department
of the task which he had to perform, and he laboured in it with un-

exhausted and uncrippled energies till the bowl was broken at the fountain ; experience visited him early, fancy lingered with him to the last; the rapid developement of his powers was an indication of the internal strength of his genius ; their steady continuance was a type and prognostic of the perpetual endurance of his sway. The cold and fiendish Gloster was an early conception; the eager Shylock and the superhuman Hamlet were imagined simultaneously not long afterwards; the tenderness of Lear was the fruit of the poet's ripest age ; and one of the closing years of his life gave birth to the savage wildness and the youthful and aerial beauty of 'The Tempest.'

Experience came soon to him; Fancy abode with him to the end.

Gloster (Ric. III.) was early, Shylock and Hamlet of middle time, Lear in ripe age,

The Tempest, near his death.

Our last words are claimed by the proper subject of our inquiry. Have I convinced you that in the composition of 'The Two Noble Kinsmen', Shakspeare had the extensive participation which I have ascribed to him ? It is very probable that my reasoning is in many parts defective ; but I place so much confidence in the goodness of the cause itself, that I would unhesitatingly leave the question, without a word of argument, to be determined by any one, possessing a familiar acquaintance with both the poets whose claims are to be balanced, and an ordinarily acute discernment of their distinguishing qualities. I am firmly persuaded that the subject needs only to have attention directed to it ; and my investigation of it cannot have been a failure in every particular. The circumstances attending the first publication of the drama do not, in the most unfavourable view which can with any fairness be taken of them, exclude us from deciding the question of Shakspeare's authorship by an examination of the work itself: and it is unnecessary that the effect of the external evidence should be estimated one step higher. Do the internal proofs allot all to Fletcher, or assign any share to Shakspeare? The Story is ill-suited for the dramatic purposes ¹of the one poet, and belongs to a class of subjects at variance with his style of thought, and not elsewhere chosen by him or any author of the school to which he belonged ; both the individual and the class accord with the whole temper and all the purposes of the other poet, and the class is one from which he has repeatedly selected themes. It

Are you convinc't that Shakspere wrote much of The Two Noble Kinsmen ?

I'm sure the question needs only attention.

The external evidence doesn't include the internal.

Does that give all the play to Fletcher?

[¹ page 110]

The Story is alien to Fletcher

Fletcher can't have chosen the subject of *The Two Noble Kinsmen*; nor was its plan his.

Its Scenical Arrangement is like Shakspere's.

Its Execution is, in great part, so like his,

that many passages must be set down to him.

Look at all the circumstances together,

and see whether the many probabilities do not make a certainty.

[' page 111]

is next to impossible that Fletcher can have selected the subject; it is not unlikely that Shakspeare may have suggested it; and if the execution of the plan shall be thought to evince that he was in any degree connected with the work, we can hardly avoid the conclusion that it was by him that the subject was chosen. The proof here, (which I think has not been noticed by any one before me,) seems to me to be stronger than in any other branch of the argument. The Scenical Arrangement of the drama offers points of resemblance to Shakspeare, which, at the very least, have considerable strength when they are taken together, and are corroborative of other circumstances. The Execution of that large proportion of the drama which has been marked off as his, presents circumstances of likeness to him, so numerous that they cannot possibly have been accidental, and so strikingly characteristic that we cannot conceive them to be the product of imitation. Even if it should be doubted whether Shakspeare chose the subject, or arranged any part of the plot, it seems to me that his claim to the authorship of these individual parts needs only examination to be universally admitted; not that I consider the proof here as stronger than that which establishes his choice of the plot, but because it is of a nature to be more easily and intuitively comprehended.

In forming your opinion, you will be careful to view the circumstances, not singly, but together, and to give each point of resemblance the support of the others. It may be that every consideration suggested may not affect your mind with equal strength of conviction; but numerous probabilities all tending the same way are sufficient to generate positive certainty: and it argues no imperfection in a result that it is brought out only by combined efforts. In those climates of the New World which you have visited, a spacious and lofty chamber receives a diffusive shower of light through a single narrow aperture, while in our cloudy region we can gather sufficient light for our apartments only by opening large and numerous windows: the end is not gained in the latter case without greater exertion than that which is required in the former, but it is attained equally in both; for the aspect of our habitations is not less cheerful than that of yours.

On the absolute merit of the work, I do not wish to anticipate your judgment. So far as Shakspeare's share in it is concerned, it can be regarded as no more than a sketch, which would be seen to great disadvantage beside finished drawings of the same master. Imperfect as it is, however, it would, if it were admitted among Shakspeare's acknowledged works, outshine many, and do discredit to none. It would be no unfair trial to compare it with those works of his in which he abstains from his more profound investigations into human nature, permitting the poetical world actively to mingle with the dramatic, and the radiant spirit of hope to embrace the sterner genius of knowledge. We may call up before us the luxurious fancies of the 'Midsummer Night's Dream', or even the sylvan landscapes of the Forest of Ardennes, and the pastoral groupes which people it ; and we shall gladly acknowledge a similar though harsher style of colouring, and a strength of contour indicating the same origin. But perhaps there is none of his works with which it could be so fairly compared as 'Henry VIII'. In the tone of sentiment and imagination, as well as in other particulars, I perceive many circumstances of likeness, which it will gratify you to trace for yourself. The resemblance is more than a fanciful one, and the neglected play does not materially suffer by the comparison.

Shakspere's part in The Two Noble Kinsmen, is but a sketch ; yet it 's better than some of his finisht works.

Compare it with the Midsummer Night's Dream ;

the colouring and outline are from the same hand. But best, set it beside Henry VIII.

It's more like that, and nearly as good.

This drama will never receive the praise which it merits, till it shall have been admitted among Shakspeare's undoubted works ; and, I repeat, it is entitled to insertion if any one of the conclusions to which I have attempted to lead you be sound,—if it be true that he wrote all, or most, or a few, of those portions of it, which more competent judges than I have already confidently ascribed to him. Farewell.

The Two Noble Kinsmen ought to be in every 'Shakspere's Works.'

W. S.

Edinburgh, March 1833.

[In his article on 'Recent Shaksperian Literature' in No. 144 of the *Edinburgh Review,* July, 1840, page 468, Prof. Spalding states that on Shakspere's taking part in *The Two Noble Kinsmen,* his "opinion is not now so decided as it once was."—F.]

A FEW INSTANCES OF SHAKSPERE'S PECULIARITIES AS NOTED BY SPALDING.

Repetition, p. 12. 1. Prologue to *Henry V.*:

> 'And at his heels,
> Leashed in like hounds, should famine, sword, and fire,
> Crouch for employment.'

Compare *Antony and Cleopatra*, Act I. scene iv. :

> ' Where thou slew'st, Hirtus and Pausa, consuls, at thy heel
> Did famine follow.'

2. *Macbeth*, Act V. scene vii. :

> ' They have tied me to a stake : I cannot fly,
> But, bear-like, I must fight the course ' ;

and *Lear*, Act III. scene vii. :

> ' I am tied to the stake, and I must stand the course.'

Conciseness verging on obscurity, p. 13.   *Macbeth*, Act I. scene iii. :

> ' Present fears are less than horrible imaginings :
> My thought, whose murder yet is but fantastical,
> Shakes so my single state of man, that function
> Is smothered in surmise, and nothing is
> But what is not.'

Act I. scene vii. :

> ' If it were done when 'tis done,' etc.

Act V. scene vii. :

> ' Now does he feel
> His secret murders sticking on his hands :
> Now minutely revolts upbraid his faith-breach ;
> Those he commands, move only in command,
> Nothing in love.'

Coriolanus, Act IV. scene vii. :

> ' Whether 'twas pride,
> Which out of daily fortune ever taints
> The happy man ; whether defect of judgement,

To fail in the disposing of those chances
Which he was lord of ; or whether nature,
Not to be other than one thing, not moving
From the casque to the cushion, but commanding peace,
Even with the same austerity and garb,
As he controlled the war ; but one of these
As he hath spices of them all, not all,
For I dare so far free him,—made him feared,
So hated, and so banished.'

Metaphors crowded with ideas, p. 17.   *Julius Cæsar*, Act II.
scene i. l. 81-4.

> 'Seek none, conspiracy.
> Hide it thy visage in smiles and affability ;
> For if thou *path*, thy native semblance on,
> Not Erebus itself were dim enough to hide thee from *prevention*.'

Macbeth, Act V. scene vii. :

> 'Meet we the medicine of the sickly weal,
> And with him pour we in our country's purge,
> Each drop of us.   Or so much as it needs
> To dew the sovereign flower and drown the weeds.'
(rather strained figures).

Hamlet, Act I. scene iv. :

> 'So, oft it chances in particular men,
> That for some *vicious mole* of nature in them,
> As, in their birth,—wherein they are not guilty,
> Since nature cannot choose his origin,
> By the *o'ergrowth* of some *complexion*,
> Oft breaking down the *pales* and *forts* of Reason,
> Or by some habit that too much o'er *leavens*
> The form of plausive manners, that these men
> Carrying, I say, the *stamp* of one defect,
> Being *nature's livery*, or *fortune's star*,—
> Their virtues else—be they as pure as grace,
> As infinite as man may undergo,—
> Shall in the general censure take *corruption*
> From that particular fault.'

Conceits and Wordplay, p. 22.   *Richard II*, Act II. scene i. :

> 'Old Gaunt indeed and gaunt in being old,' etc.

Love's Labour's Lost, Act IV. scene iii. :

> 'They have pitched a toil, I am toiling in a pitch !'

Personification, p. 25.   *Two Gentlemen*, Act I. scene i. :
'So *eating Love*
Inhabits in the finest wits of all.'

Richard II, Act III. scene ii. :
'Foul *Rebellion's* arms.'

Midsummer Night's Dream :
'The debt that *bankrupt Sleep* doth Sorrow owe.'

Henry V, Act II. scene ii. :
'*Treason* and *Murder* ever kept together.'

Macbeth, Act I. scene iii. :
'If *Chance* will have me king,
Why *Chance* may crown me.'

Act II. scene i. :
'*Witchcraft* celebrates
Pale Hecate's offerings, and withered *Murder*,
Alarmed by his sentinel, the wolf.'

Troilus and Cressida, Act III. scene iii. :
'*Welcome* ever smiles,
And *Farewell* goes out sighing.'

---

p. v. *Marigolds.* Dr Prior, writing from his place, Halse, near Taunton, 11 Oct., 1876, says, "I asked in a family here whether they had ever heard of marigolds being strown on the beds of dying persons, and they referred me to a book by Lady C. Davies, *Recollections of Society*, 1873. At p. 129:

"'Is Little Trianon ominous to crowned women?'

"'Passing through the garden,' said the King, 'I perceived some *soucis* (marigolds, emblems of sorrow and care) growing near a tuft of lilies. This coincidence struck me, and I murmured :

"Dans les jardins de Trianon
Je cueillais des roses nouvelles.
Mais, helas ! les fleurs les plus belles
Avaient péri sous les glaçons.
J'eus beau chercher les dons de Flore,
Les hivers les avaient detruits ;
Je ne trouvai que des *soucis*
Qu'humectaient les pleurs de l'Aurore." '

"I am inclined to hold my first opinion that *cradle* and *death-bed* refer to the use of the flowers, and not to anything in their growth or appearance."

p. 1. *My dear L—*.   Altho' Prof. Spalding says that L. was an early and later friend of his, of great gifts and taste, and that he had visited the New World (p. 108), yet Mrs Spalding and Dr Burton have never been able to identify L., and they believe him to be a creation of the author's.—F.

p. 4. *Shakspere had fallen much into neglect by* 1634.   "After the death of Shakspeare, the plays of Fletcher appear for several years to have been more admired, or at least to have been more frequently acted, than those of our poet." Malone, *Hist. Account of the English Stage*, Variorum Shakspere of 1821, vol. ii. p. 224.   And see the lists following, by which he proves his statement.—F.

From the Paper with which Mr J. Herbert Stack opend the discussion at our Reading of the *Two Noble Kinsmen*, he has allowd me to make the following extracts :—

"To judge the question clearly, let us note how far the author or authors of the *Two N. K.* followed what was the basis of their drama—Chaucer's Knightes Tale. We have there the same opening incident—the petitions of the Queens, then the capture of the Two, then their sight of Emily from the prison window, the release of Arcite, his entry into Emilia's service, the escape of Palamon, the fight in the wood, the decree of Theseus, the prayers to Diana, Venus, and Mars, the combat, the victory in arms to Arcite, his death, and Palamon's eventual victory in love. But Chaucer is far superior to the dramatists.   He has no Gaoler's Daughter to distract our thoughts.   The language of his Palamon is more blunt, more soldier-like, more characteristic.   His Emilia, instead of being equally in love with two men at the same time, prefers maidenhood to marriage, loves neither, but pities both.   At the end of the *play* we have something coarse and hurried : Emilia, during the Tournament, is ready to jump into anybody's arms, so that he comes victorious ; then she accepts Arcite ; and on his sudden death, she dries her tears with more than the supposed celerity of a modern fashionable widow ; and, before she is the widow of Arcite, consents to become the wife of Palamon.   Contrast this with Chaucer, where the poem dedicates some beautiful lines to the funeral of Arcite and the grief of all, and only makes Emilia yield after years to the silent pleading of the woful Palamon and the urgency of her brother.   Contrast the dying speeches in the two works.   In the play, Arcite transfers Emilia almost as if he were making a will : "*Item*, I leave my bride to Palamon."   In Chaucer, he says to Emilia that he knows of no man

> ' So worthy to be loved as Palamon,
> And if that you shal ever be a wyf
> Forget not Palamon that gentil man.'

Now here we have a play founded on a poem, the original delicate and noble, where the other is coarse and trivial ; and we ask, ' Was this Shakspere's way of treating his originals ?'   In his earlier years he based his *Romeo and Juliet* on Brooke's poem of the same name—a fine work, and little disfigured by the coarseness of the time.   Yet he pruned it of all really offensive matter, and has given us a perfect love-story, as ardent as it is pure.   His skill in omission is remarkably shown in one respect.   In Brooke's poem, Juliet, reflecting when alone on Romeo's sudden love, remembers that he is an enemy to her house, and suspects that he

SPALDING.   8 may intend dishonourable love as a base means of wreaking vengeance on hereditary foes. It seems to me that a thought so cunning is out of character with Juliet—certainly would have been felt as a stain on Shakspere's Juliet. That Shakspere deliberately omitted this, is known by one slight reference. Juliet says to Romeo,

> 'If thy intent of love be honourable,
> Thy purpose marriage.'

That is all—no cunning caution, no base doubt.

Now if in this original, and in this play, we trace the very manner of Shakspere's working—taking up gold mixed with dross, and purifying it in the furnace of his genius—are we to suppose that later in life, with taste more fastidious, even if his imagination were less strong, he carried out a converse process ; that he took Chaucer's gold, and mixed it with alloy? That, I greatly doubt. Also, would he imitate himself so closely as he is imitated in certain scenes of the *Two N. K.* ?

Another point. Love between persons of very different rank has been held by many dramatists to be a fine subject for the stage. Shakspere never introduces it. *Ophelia* loves a Prince, and *Violet* a duke, and Rosalind a Squire's son ; but gentlehood unites all. Helena in *All's Well* is a gentlewoman. With anything like levelling aspirations Shakspere had clearly no sympathy. In no undoubted play of his have we, so far as I remember, any attempt to make the love of the lowly born for the high a subject of sympathy : there is no Beggar maid to any of his King Cophetuas. Goneril and Regan stoop to Edmund through baseness ; Malvolio's love for Olivia is made ridiculous. The Gaoler's Daughter of the *Two N. K.* stands alone : like the waiting-maid in the *Critic*, she goes mad in white linen, and as painfully recalls Ophelia, as our cousins the monkeys remind us of men.

In some other respects the poem is far superior to the play. Chaucer introduces the supernatural powers with excellent effect and tact—so as to soften the rigour of the Duke's decrees. In the Temple, Palamon, the more warlike in manners of the two, is the more reckless and ardent in his love : of a simpler nature, Venus entirely subdues and, at the same time, effectually befriends him. He prays to her not for Victory : for that he cares not : it matters not how events are brought about 'so that I have my lady in mine arms.' Arcite, the softer and more refined knight, prays simply for Victory. If it be true that love changes the nature of men, here we have the transformation. The prayer of each is granted, though they seem opposed—thus Arcite experiences what many of those who consulted old oracles found, 'the word of promise kept to the ear, broken to the hope.' Then in the poem Theseus freely forgives the two knights, but decides on the Tournament as a means of seeing who shall have Emilia. In the play he decides that one is to live and marry, the other to die. The absurdity of this needless cruelty is evident : it was possibly introduced to satisfy the coarse tastes of the audiences who liked the sight of an executioner and a block.

In fact I would say the play is not mainly Shakspere's because of its un-Shaksperean depth. Who can sympathize with the cold, coarse balancing of Emilia between the two men—eager to have one, ready to take either ; betrothed in haste to one, married in haste to another—so far flying in the face of the pure beauty of the original, where Emilia never loses maidenly reserve. Then the final marriage of the Gaoler's Daughter is as destructive of our sympathy as if Ophelia had been saved from drowning by the grave-digger, and married to Horatio at the end of the piece. The pedantry of Gerrold is poor, the fun of the rustics forced and feeble, the sternness of Theseus brutal and untouched by final gentleness as in Chaucer.

Another argument against Shakspere's responsibility for the whole play is the manner in which the minor characters are introduced and the underplot managed. A secondary plot is a characteristic of the Elizabethan drama, borrowed from that of Spain. But Shakspere is peculiar in the skill with which he interweaves the two plots and brings together the principal and the inferior personages. In *Hamlet* the soldiers on the watch, the grave-diggers, the players, the two walking gentlemen, even Osric, all help on the action of the drama and come into relation with the hero himself. In *King Lear*, Edmund and Gloster and Edgar, though engaged in a subsidiary drama of their own, get mixed up with the fortunes of the King and his daughters. In *Othello*, the foolish Venetian Roderigo and Bianca the courtesan have some hand in the progress of the play. In *Romeo and Juliet*, the Nurse and the Friar are agents of the main plot, and the ball scene pushes on the action. In *Shylock*, Lancelot Gobbo is servant to the Jew, and helps Jessica to escape. I need not multiply instances, as in *Much Ado about Nothing*, Dogberry, &c. As far as my own recollection serves, I do not believe that in any play undoubtedly Shakspere's we have a single instance of an under-plot like that of the Gaoler's Daughter. It might be altogether omitted without affecting the story. Theseus, Emilia, Hippolyta, Arcite, Palamon, never exchange a word with the group of Gaoler's Daughter, Wooer, Brother, two Friends and Doctor ; and Palamon's only remembrance of her services is that at his supposed moment of execution he generously leaves her the money he had no further need of to help her to get married to a remarkably tame young man who assumes the name of his rival in order to bring his sweetheart to her senses. If this underplot is due to Shakspere, why is there none like it in all his works? If these exceedingly thin and very detached minor characters are his, where in his undoubted plays are others like them—thus hanging loosely on to the main machinery of a play? Nor must we forget that if this underplot is Shakspere's, it is his when he was an experienced dramatist—so that after being a skilful constructor and connecter of plot and underplot in his youth, 'his right hand forgot its cunning' in his middle age.

Two other arguments. In the Prologue of the play, written and recited when it was acted, there are two passages expressing great fears as to the result,—one that Chaucer might rise to condemn the dramatist for spoiling his story,—another that the play might be damned, and destroy the fortunes of the Theatre[1]. Is this the way in which a play partly written by Shakspere—then near the close of his successful stage career—would be spoken of on its production?

Another argument is, if Shakspere, using Chaucer's poem as a model, spoiled it in dramatising it[2], then as a poet he was inferior to Chaucer—which is absurd.

---

[1] Does not this as much imply that Fletcher knew he had spoiled what Shakpere would have done well ?—H. L.

[2] But this is confessedly the case with Chaucer's *Troilus.*—F. [Not quite. In

Following high authorities, anybody may adopt any opinion on this play and find backers—the extremes being the German Tieck, who entirely rejects the idea of Shakspere's authorship, and Mr Hickson, who throws on him the responsibility for the whole framework of a play and the groundwork of every character. I should incline to the middle opinion[1], that Shakspere selected the subject, began the play, wrote many passages ; had no underplot, and generally left it in a skeleton state ; that Fletcher took it up, patched it here and there, and added an underplot ;—that Fletcher, not Shakspere, is answerable for all the departures from Chaucer, for all the underplot, and for the revised play as it stands. There is nothing improbable in this. After Shakspere retired to Stratford, Fletcher may have found the play amongst the MSS. of the Theatre, and then produced it after due changes made—not giving the author's name. At that time it was the custom that a play remained the property of the company of actors who produced it. That the Blackfriars Company did *not* regard the play as Shakspere's is pretty plain—for in the edition of 1623, published by Heminge and Condell of that company, Shakspere's own fellow-players, the play is not included. Nor does the part authorship account for the omission, as plays with less of Shakspere's undoubted authorship are there included. But the omission is intelligible if the play had been so Fletcherised that it was, when acted, generally regarded as Fletcher's. Fletcher was alive in 1623 to claim all as his property ; but in 1634 he was dead. Then the publisher, knowing or hearing that Shakspere had a share, printed *his* name, after *Fletcher's*, as part dramatist. Thus I return to the older verdict of Coleridge and Lamb, that Shakspere wrote passages of this play, perhaps also the outlines, but that Fletcher filled up, added an underplot, and finally revised.

Troilus the travestie is intentional : in the *Two N. K.* Chaucer is solemnly Cibberised.—J. H. S.]

[1] Also my view—though I hesitate to express a firm opinion on the matter—PERHAPS Shakspere worked on the 1594 play as a basis?—H. L.

INDEX.

ALFIERI. His intensity, p. 91.

Apollo, the statue, 87.

As you like it, 75, 100.

BEAUMONT. Partnership with Fletcher, 2, 5, 6, 62, 63, 73.

Beautiful, the, in Art, 85, 89.

Bridal Song in *Two Noble Kinsmen*, 27.

Characterization, Shakspere's, 94.

CHAUCER. Correspondences in the *Two Noble Kinsmen* with the *Knight's Tale*, 40, 45, 53 ; differences from it, 35, 39, 44, 48, 54 ; his classical subjects, 65, 66 ; influence on Shakspere, 67, 68, 72 ; school founded by him, 67 ; version of the story, 26.

Classical allusions in contemporary writers, 18, 19.

Classical mythology in Shakspere, 19 ; poetry, 71 ; story, 64.

Contemporary dramatists. Their licentiousness, 102 ; points in common with Shakspere, 56, 57 ; representations of passion, 95, 96 ; stage effects, 74 ; subjects, 63, 73.

DANTE, 91.

Date of the *Two Noble Kinsmen* 1634, 4.

Didactic poetry, 92.

Editors, Shakspere's first, 6-8.

Epic poetry, 92.

Evidence as to authorship of the *Two N. K.*, Historical, 3—5 ; Internal, 10—25.

Fine art, 86.

FLETCHER. His co-authors, 5, 6 ; diffuseness and elaboration, 14 ; differences between him and Shakspere, 57 ; his 'men of pleasure,' 42, 102 ; popularity, 4 ; plots 63, 66 ; poverty in metaphor, 17, and in thought, compared with Shakspere, 20, 21. His rhythm, 11 : his share in the *Two Noble Kinsmen* : all second act, five scenes in third act, all fourth act, one scene in fifth act, 35—40, 42- 45, 59 ; his slowness of association, 37 ; vague, ill-graspt imagery, 16, 36 ; want of personification, 25 ; wit, 23.

Folios, Shakspere's first and second, 6—9.

FORD. Choice of plots, 74 ; 'Death of Annabella,' 80.

Greek arts of design, poetry contrasted with modern, 71, 83.

Hamlet, 94, 104, 106.

Henry VIII, 109.

Imagination, 90, 93.

Invention defind by Alfieri, 92 *n.*

Jailer's daughter, 61.

Jaques, 100, 101.

JOHNSON, Dr Sam, 102.

JONSON, BEN. Comparative failure in delineating passion, 95, 96 ; his plots and Shakspere's, 36, 62, 73 ; his humour, 23 ; his likeness to Shakspere, 57 ; partnership with Fletcher, 6 ; 'Sejanus' untoucht by Shakspere, 2.

Laocoon, the sculpture, 87.

Lear, the end of, 76, 94, 99.

LESSING'S *Laocoon*, 83 ; principles of plastic art, 83, 86.

LODGE, 64.

LYLY. His faults, 22.

www.ingramcontent.com/pod-product-compliance
Lightning Source LLC
Chambersburg PA
CBHW030606270326
41927CB00007B/1059